WRITING GENRE FLASH FICTION
THE MINIMALIST WAY

A SELF-STUDY BOOK

Michael A. Kechula

BooksForABuck.com
2011

Michael A. Kechula

BooksForABuck.com
January 2011
ISBN: 978-1-60215-137-6

ABOUT THIS BOOK

Welcome. The purpose of this book is to teach you how to develop genre flash fiction the minimalist way. The contents are based on what we taught dozens of novelists and short story authors when we transformed them into genre flash writers.

In a few moments, we'll define flash fiction, genre fiction, and the minimalist approach to developing flash. Before we do, here's how we'll proceed with the lessons. First, we'll tell you something and show some examples. Then we'll ask you questions. All questions begin with Q followed by a number. Many involve word reduction writing exercises. Have a pencil on hand to answer the questions and complete the exercises. Write your answers in the places provided.

Answers to all questions and exercises appear in the Answer Pages at the back of the book.

Also included is a 50 question Word Reduction Exercise to give you more practice in writing tighter sentences. Answers for the questions appear in the Word Reduction Answer Pages, which appear at the back of the book.

The book contains 10 lessons. We suggest you review Lesson-1, and Lesson-2 first. Then you may review the rest in any sequence. The lesson names and page numbers are listed in the menu on the next page.

To save space from this point forward, we'll use the abbreviation FF to mean flash fiction.

This concludes the introduction. The next page shows the lesson Menu.

MENU

LESSON-1: INTRODUCTION TO GENRE FLASH FICTION

This lesson covers the following:

- Definition of FF

- Characteristics of the ideal genre FF tale

- Definition of genre fiction

- Genre names

- Objectives of the minimalist way of writing FF

- Key minimalist authoring techniques

- Definition of word-wasters

- List of word-wasters

DEFINITION OF FLASH FICTION: *a complete story told in 1,000 words or less.*

Notice we said *a complete story* and that it must be told *in 1,000 words or less.*

The severe word count limitation of flash contrasts sharply with short stories that consist of 1,000 to 10,000 words, and even more so with novels that range from 40,000 upward. But there's another and greater difference that impacts authors: flash is not developed using the same techniques for writing short stories and novels. That means authors will have to learn and apply new ones. Some flash techniques will even conflict with those authors use to develop novels and short stories. Here's an example: when writing FF from the minimalist approach, we omit similes. These figures of speech are never vital to the plot in FF stories, plus they burn up precious word count. Further, some are so poorly conceived they draw attention to themselves and throw us out of the story. This has happened hundreds of times while we were analyzing and critiquing more than 6,000 FF stories.

If you're an author of short stories or novels, we ask you to suspend any preconceived notions you have about developing genre FF. If you can do this, your transformation into a FF writer will be much easier.

Q01: What's the maximum number of words allowable in a FF tale?

_____

Q02: How does the word count available in flash compare to that of short stories and novels? Short Stories_____
Novels_____

Q03: When developing flash, we said you should omit_____

Q04: Give one reason for doing that?

Q05: What did we say about similes and how they affect the plot of a flash tale?

CHARACTERISTICS OF THE IDEAL GENRE FF STORY

The ideal genre FF tale has the following characteristics:

- It should tell a complete story that can be read in 5 minutes or less.

- It should have an opener that pulls readers into the story.

- It should be plot-driven.

- It should emphasize telling over showing.

- It should be a fast read.

- It should always move forward at a brisk pace.

- It should be free of inflated prose.

- It should be free of trivial details.

- It should be free of distractions that can throw readers out of the story.

- It should contain dialog.

- It should contain a maximum of 4 characters.

- It should contain a maximum of 4 scenes.

- It should end in a way that makes it complete.

Q06: List at least 6 characteristics of the ideal genre flash fiction story.

DEFINITION OF GENRE FICTION

Here's a dictionary description of genre, when applied to fiction: *a category of fiction characterized by a particular style, form or content.*

Here's a partial list of genre names:

- Crime

- Mystery

- Romance

- Speculative

- Thriller

- War

- Western

To see more genre names, access Google and enter: *fiction genres*

Each of the genres listed above are further divided into subgenres. For example, two subgenres of fantasy are magical realism and urban fantasy. To obtain a full list of, say, fantasy subgenres, Google on: *fantasy subgenres.*

Q07: Genre fiction is characterized by a particular style, form, or

_____

Q08: List 3 of the genre names.

The FF format works for any genre. However, the genre in greatest demand by publishers is speculative fiction. Speculative fiction is an umbrella term for sci-fi, fantasy, and horror, as well as their dozens of subgenres.

The most compelling genre fiction tales have a protagonist with a quest, and one or more antagonists who do all they can to prevent him from attaining the object of the quest. Crime tales are a good example. Romance tales can also have these elements of genre fiction. Same with adventure, fantasy, and even humorous stories. The trick is to make all this happen in 1,000 words or less.

Here's a summary of what we covered so far:

- Definition of FF

- Definition of genre fiction

- Characteristics of the ideal genre FF tale

- Genre fiction names

Let's move on to the objectives of the minimalist way of developing genre FF fiction....

OBJECTIVES OF THE MINIMALIST WAY

The objectives of the minimalist approach to writing genre FF are: *to tell as much story as possible, in as few words as possible, without sacrificing a smooth read.*

These objectives will affect how you'll begin your story, how you'll develop narrative and dialog, and how you'll edit the results before submitting to magazines, anthologies, or contests.

Q09: What are the objectives of the minimalist approach to developing FF?

```



```

Let's look more closely at the implications of these objectives. We're already constrained by a rule that says we only have 1,000 words to tell a story. That's difficult enough for any author. Now it might seem as if we're making things even tougher by asking you be stingy with words. What we're asking you to do is adapt 4 minimalist techniques to meet the objectives, which are:

- Write tight sentences.

- Tell, not show.

- Make stories plot-driven.

- Omit word-wasters.

Let's look more closely at these techniques…

WRITE TIGHT SENTENCES

This means you should eliminate superfluous words in every sentence in the story. Sometimes this might involve removing a single word, such as *the, that, and.*

Tightly written sentences make the story move forward faster. However, when you tighten a sentence, always make sure the result reads smoothly. You can tell by reading the sentence aloud before you make the change, and again after. Keep the sentence that sounds best.

Here's an example of a sentence that isn't written as tightly as it can be: *Mother first told me about the haunted house when I was ten years old.*

We can tighten this sentence by cutting 2 words: *years, old.* After the deletion, the sentence becomes: *Mother first told me about the haunted house when I was ten.* Notice that deleting 2 words hasn't changed the meaning of the sentence.

Here's another example: *John felt sorry for the kid who didn't have any money.*

Removing *any* doesn't change the meaning: *John felt sorry for the kid who didn't have money.*

Another example: *When Charlie found out about it, he screamed at her.*

Deleting *about it* gives us: *When Charlie found out, he screamed at her.*

More examples...

BEFORE: *Liz stowed the box away under the counter.*

AFTER: *Liz stowed the box under the counter.*

BEFORE: *The kids all cheered, because they loved ice cream.*

AFTER: *The kids cheered, because they loved ice cream.*

BEFORE: *Although most of the shoppers avoided the pamphleteers, Joe walked directly up to them and took one of their pamphlets.*

AFTER: *Although most shoppers avoided the pamphleteers, Joe took one of their pamphlets.*

We cut *walked directly up to then and* because the only way he could take a pamphlet was to do that. Therefore, it's understood and doesn't have to be included in the sentence.

Q10: Tighten this a bit: *She reached out and took a blade to see how sharp it was.*

Q11: Delete whatever's necessary to tighten this: *The girl grew very curious, but her grandmother wouldn't let her open the box or even to touch it.*

Q12: Tighten this sentence: *He said goodbye to Deborah, and headed out the door.* HINT: This needs to be rewritten.

Q13: Make this tighter: *She started to sort the mail.*

Q14: Why should your sentences be as tight as possible when developing FF?

You may be surprised at the number of words you can cut from your first draft without affecting the meaning of the story. Remember the less words, the faster the read.

This book includes dozens of word-reduction exercises to give you practice in detecting and removing superfluous words.

TELL, NOT SHOW

Writing the minimalist way means you'll have to place far more emphasis on telling than showing in the narrative. Showing is a neat option when you have thousands of words available to tell a story. However, it becomes an impediment to FF development, because more words are needed to show than tell. For example, if we want to show readers that a female character is well-dressed, we could burn up quite a bit of word count describing her outfit from top to bottom, including colors, and names of high-fashion designers on the tags. Authors might use dozens of words to get this image across to readers. With little effort, it's possible to expend 100 words, or 10% of the available word count in a 1,000-word tale just to portray a very simple idea: a woman was well dressed.

If authors continuously show in the narrative, such as describing her custom-made car, her apartment, what her table setting looks like, they'll find they've run out of word count before the tale is finished. The moment authors add one word beyond 1,000, the work is no longer FF—it becomes a short story.

In contrast, by telling the reader *the woman was well-dressed*, expends only 4 words, considering *well-dressed* counts as one word.

The emphasis on telling in flash doesn't mean you'll have to give up showing entirely. You'll still be able to show many things about characters through carefully crafted dialog.

Q15: When it comes to showing or telling, which approach is preferable in the narrative of a minimalist FF tale?

_____.

Q16: Why is telling preferable to showing when developing FF?

Q17: _____ can be used to show many things about characters.

MAKE STORIES PLOT-DRIVEN

Plot-driven stories require far less word count than character-driven stories. If you're not sure of the differences been the two, consider the following:

- In plot-driven stories, events take precedence.

- In character-driven stories, characters take precedence.

Q18: Because of word count limitations, FF tales are _____-driven.

Q19: In a plot-driven story, _____ take precedence.

OMIT WORD-WASTERS

We define a word-waster as any word, sentence, or paragraph included in a FF tale that isn't vital to the plot. Including word-wasters prevents authors from achieving minimalist objectives. Consequently, it's a key concept of the minimalist approach.

Here's an example of a word-waster: an author interrupts the action in a fast-moving bank robbery scene to tell us the teller's hair color. A minimalist would not do this, because a character's hair color in a story about a bank robbery is superfluous to the plot.

We've seen instances where 60% of the total word count in a single FF story was expended on wasted words. This occurs when authors approach FF as if they were developing a short story or novel.

Everybody includes wasted words to some extent when developing the first draft of a FF story. However, the important things are to recognize and delete them. This may involve rewriting the affected sentences. We'll cover this in detail in Lessons 5 through 10.

Below is an example of what we mean by word-wasters. It consists of narrative we extracted from a FF tale. Each line was included with the story's dialog. The story consisted of 641 words, of which 166 were completely superfluous to the plot. Thus, 26% of the story's total word count was nothing more than fluff and filler, none of which was vital to the plot.

The 166 superfluous words we extracted are shown below in the sequence in which they appeared. To save space, we substituted A and B for character names.

- She shoved A forward.

- A barked, barely keeping her balance.

- The man flashed a smile that didn't quite reach his eyes and held out his hand to the table.

- A shrugged.

- The man nodded.

- A snorted. She whirled around to regard B over her shoulder.

- The man sighed.

- A shrugged again.

- Demonstrating, A mirrored his movements.

- She chirped.

- He smirked.

- A looked up from her cell phone.

- She turned her attention back to the man.

- The man frowned.

- Suddenly, the man gasped.

- He looked from A to B and back again.

- A pouted.

- She got up from her cushion and slid her cell phone back into her pocket.

- Folded her arms across her chest.

- B frowned.

- She started to span the gap between them, her heels turning up divots of spring mud behind her.

- The man leaned over, his face red.

- The man looked her up and down and sighed.

- He gave her a steely look.

- A began to smile.

- B beamed at him.

You just saw a list of actions that characters did while they spoke. This includes: shoved, barked, flashed, held out, shrugged, nodded, snorted (twice), demonstrated, chirped, smirked, looked up, turned, frowned (twice), gasped, looked, got up, slid, folded, started, gave, began, beamed.

You'll find FF tales loaded with trivial details like this in every story not developed the minimalist way. Filling a story with this kind of writing prevents authors from telling the most story possible in as few words as possible.

Not everything that follows a line of dialog is a word-waster. Here's an example: *"Give me my split of the bank job, or I'll blow your head off." He grabbed his pistol.*

In this case, the words, or action tags, following the dialog are vital to the plot. We now have the idea that somebody may get shot.

On the other hand, if we'd said this, we would've wasted words: *"Give me my split of the bank job, or I'll blow your head off," he said, wrinkling his nose and shifting a few inches forward in his hard, wooden chair.*

The words in this example are wasted, because FF readers don't care what the speaker did with his nose, or that he shifted forward in a chair. Nor do they care how far forward the speaker shifted, and the fact that the chair was hard and made of wood. Readers are expecting to read about significant events, not reports of nose wrinkles and body shifting.

When FF authors include such trivial details, the only thing they accomplish is to force readers to focus on insignificant mannerisms. In FF, that only slows down the read and makes the story boring.

Keep pitfalls like this in mind while developing your story. Be a storyteller first and writer second. Remember: writers who aren't storytellers tend to include fluff, but storytellers who are writers don't.

Here's a summary of what we covered in this lesson:

- Definition of FF

- Characteristics of the ideal genre FF tale

- Definition of genre fiction

- Genre names

- Objectives of the minimalist way of writing FF

- 4 minimalist techniques to meet the objectives:

    - Write tight sentences.

    - Tell, not show.

    - Make stories plot-driven, not character driven.

    - Omit word-wasters.

- Definition of word-wasters

- Examples of word-wasters

This concludes Lesson-1.

LESSON-2

GENRE FF DEVELOPMENT PROCESS

This lesson includes the following:

- Overview of the genre FF development process.

- Tips for naming characters.

- Counting words in a FF tale.

- Editing your first draft.

- List of dialog word-wasters.

- List of narrative word-wasters.

- Example of a prize-winning FF tale developed the minimalist way.

- How minimalist techniques were applied to the sample story.

OVERVIEW OF THE DEVELOPMENT PROCESS

Here's a summary of the major FF development tasks:

TASK 1: Have a story idea ready for development.

TASK 2: Write the story the minimalist way.

TASK 3: Count the words in the story.

TASK 4: Read the draft to determine needed fixes.

TASK 5: Edit the draft to make fixes.

TASK 6: Repeat 3 through 5 until the manuscript is ready for submission.

Let's review these steps...

TASK 1: HAVE A STORY READY FOR DEVELOPMENT

The first thing you'll need is an idea that can be developed into a FF tale. Do you already have one?

> If YES... ...skip forward to Writing Your Story The Minimalist Way on the next page.

> If NO... ...continue reading.

Here are some tips on how to find story ideas:

- Join a flash fiction writing group that issues prompts. A very helpful one is FlashXer, a Yahoo writing group in which 3 prompts are issued weekly.
- Check online news sites for unusual stories.
- Keep a notebook and pen handy, in case a story idea pops into your mind.
- Use a voice recorder to capture your thoughts as they occur. We keep 4 handy in strategic places.
- Use a voice recorder to generate ideas from your unconscious. Pick a word, such as alien. Say the word 10 times. Without censoring, say whatever comes to your mind. You may find terrific ideas bubbling to the surface.
- Check the Internet for story ideas by entering these search words on Google: *story ideas.*
- Try writing the worst possible opening sentence for a story. Surprisingly, this often gives the opposite result.

TASK 2: WRITING THE STORY THE MINIMALIST WAY

We suggest you write the story using the same words you'd use when telling it to a friend over coffee.

For example, suppose you want to tell him about a new idea you had. Would you start telling him like this? *"When I woke up this morning, a signal flare of an idea lit my mind."*

Or would you say this? *"When I woke up this morning, I suddenly got a great idea."*

No doubt, you'd use the words shown in the second sentence. That's the storyteller's way or relating a story, while the first sentence is the writer's way.

You can't help but notice the startling differences between the two.

Let's say you now want to tell your friend you grabbed a notebook and wrote down the idea, so you wouldn't forget it. Would you tell him in these words? *"I reached for my blue-colored Bic pen with its padded surface to cushion my forefinger and thumb, took in a deep breath, coughed, and wrote my idea down."*

Or would you say this? *"I grabbed my note book and wrote it down."*

Once again we see the differences between both ways of telling the story. One is direct and to the point, and the other is loaded with trivial details your friend won't care about. In fact, if you continued to speak in such a round-about way, your friend might get impatient and as ask you cut the fluff and get to the point. That's exactly what we are asking you to do when you develop FF tales. The only sure way to do that is to adapt the minimalist approach.

Keep this in mind when you get a story idea and want to write it on paper or type it into a computer file. You may be tempted to tell the story the way a writer would, not the way a storyteller would. As you see, there's quite a difference between both methods of delivery. Therefore, we suggest you think of yourself as a storyteller first and writer second.

TIPS FOR NAMING CHARACTERS

Consider the following when naming characters the minimalist way:

- Use only first names, unless the characters are famous. Readers don't care about last names in such short pieces. Plus, last names waste one word each time they appear with a first name. The other option is to use only last names.
- Use simple names. For example, use the first letters of the alphabet in sequence to name characters when there are more than two. This helps readers to more easily distinguish between them. Examples: Ann, Barb, Clara, Donna for women. Art, Bill, Carl, Dan, for men.

- Avoid complicated spellings if you use a character's last name instead of a first name. For example: Bollyn, Bourbonne, Carlisle, de Kuyper, Kounekakis, Kaczmarczyk. Pucciavenicelli. Names like this throw readers out of the story.
- Avoid complicated titles for characters. For example: Count of the Realm Porchinski, His Royal and Most Worthy Highness King Polycarp, Lady-in-Waiting Philomena, Professor Doctor Schildkraut. Note how many words they require.
- Avoid ridiculous names, unless the work is satirical.

Q20: Why do we omit last names in FF?

Q21: What problem arises when you include a last name with a complicated spelling?

TASK 3: COUNT THE WORDS IN THE FIRST DRAFT

Use your word processor to count the words in your draft. If you've exceeded 1,000 you'll have to edit your work until you reach that number or lower.

If you intend to submit to magazines, anthologies, or contests, take note of the following:

- Always run a word count program before submitting your story.
- Some publications and contests limit the number of words you can use for the title. Their guidelines specify the maximum they'll accept.
- Titles aren't included in word counts, unless specified by guidelines.
- Count hyphenated words as 1 word. Example: well-written counts as 1 word. However, do a spell check to ensure your hyphenated words are valid.

- Count words preceded or followed by an ellipsis as 1 word each. Here's an example that was meant to portray slow, faltering speech: "You...want...ride...in...jeep...with...zombie?"
- Some editor programs will count this string of 7 words as only 1 word. To get the correct word count, remove the ellipsis between each character, run the word count program, then insert the ellipses again.
- Don't exceed the maximum word count specified by magazines, anthologies, and contests.
- Some magazines and contests require a specific word count. Ensure your submission contains the exact number of words they seek. One word more or less will invalidate your submission.

TASK 5: EDIT DRAFT TO DETERMINE NEEDED FIXES

This critical activity can make or break your story. We suggest you edit your work ruthlessly. Delete every word that prevents the story from attaining the minimalist objectives. To do this, you must scrutinize your work to see if it contains any word-wasting fillers. Here's a list of what to look for in dialog and narrative.

DIALOG WORD-WASTERS

- Action tags

- Words that can be converted to contractions

- Repetition

- Unnecessary Interruptions

- Slang

- Foreign words

- Regional dialects

- Idiomatic expressions

- Said bookisms

- Descriptions of how characters speak

Q22: Name 4 word-wasters that may occur in dialog.

NARRATIVE WORD WASTERS

- Trivial details

- Inflated prose

- Similes

- Long sentences

- Repetition

- Facts of existence

- Telling then correcting

- Telling what isn't

- Flashbacks

- Cookbook procedures

- Sluggish movements

- Superfluous pauses

- Turning

- Watching and glancing

- Impossible mannerisms

Q23: Name 6 word-wasters that could occur in the story's narrative.

We'll detail all of these word-wasters in Lessons 5 though 10. By the time you complete this book, you should be able to recognize and delete word-wasters, and rewrite sentences that contain them.

Some tips when reading your draft...

- Read it aloud. There's a difference between reading it silently and out loud. You'll notice it when you try it.

- Have a pencil and paper available to note anything you may wish to change.

- Use a voice recorder for your first reading. Play it back as many times as you wish. The more you listen to it, the more likely you are to find things that can be improved.

Now, we'll show you a FF tale...

EXAMPLE OF FF DEVELOPED THE MINIMALIST WAY

So far, we've discussed definitions, ideals, and procedures. Now we'll show you a 962-word FF story developed the minimalist way. It won second prize in a humorous horror writing contest.

A GOOD FEED

"Chief Carter, I want answers and I want them now! Who's tearing the heads off our beautiful female citizens and eating them?" asked the Mayor.

"I think it's a zombie."

"That's nuts. Werewolves, vampires—those I can understand. But zombies? That's stretching it."

"I sent the killer's MO to police agencies worldwide," said Carter. "The only answer I got was from Dr. Dumont, Head of the Haitian Zombie Institute. He said a zombie escaped from their research lab a month ago.

A vicious monster that feeds on the heads of pretty women. And get this: it likes chocolate chip cookies."

"Sounds bizarre," said the mayor. "How could a zombie get here from Haiti?"

"Maybe it got to Mexico, then paid a coyote to sneak it across the border."

"What if the missing zombie's the culprit. How can we stop it?"

"Set a trap," said the Chief. I'd like to use your wife as bait."

"Are you crazy?"

"She's the best looking woman in town. We can use her to lure the thing. Then my men will jump it with nets."

"No way! I don't want a zombie attacking my wife."

"He won't get near her. We'll put her in a gorilla cage on Main Street. She'll be real safe. Even King Kong couldn't break those bars. My men will hide in the shadows. When we catch the thing, I'll give you the pleasure of killing it—after the news conference where you'll make it sound like you captured it all by yourself. That'll ensure your reelection."

"I doubt my wife would do it. And how do you kill a zombie?"

"With a chain saw."

"Aw, hell. I can't stand the sight of blood."

"Don't worry, Mayor. Dumont said this zombie doesn't have any blood. It's filled with green gunk. The worst that can happen is that you'll get green zombie crud all over your clothes. Ain't that worth reelection?"

"Yeah. But let's keep my wife out of this. Hey, what about using that kid we crowned Miss Pumpkin Festival? She'd make perfect zombie bait."

"She ain't eighteen yet. Using her could cause big legal headaches for the city."

"Well, who can we get? Who's good looking and brave enough to sit inside a cage in the middle of the night, waiting to be attacked by a zombie?"

"Officer Crouch ain't scared of nothing. Offer her a promotion, and I'll bet she'll volunteer."

"But she looks like she was French kissed by a bulldozer," said the Mayor. "If I was a woman-eating zombie and saw her, I'd lose my appetite and run all the way back to Haiti."

"We could put a Marilyn Monroe mask on her."

"Wouldn't the zombie know and look for somebody else?"

"Not if she's in a cage at night under dim streetlights."

"Hmm," the Mayor said. "Sounds like it might work. On the other hand, you said it likes chocolate chip cookies. Why don't we forget the caged woman idea and buy a bunch of cookies. We can put one every couple of feet to form trails leading to a humongous cookie pile on Main Street. When the zombie reaches the pile, your men could jump it."

"Good idea, Mayor. I'll send somebody to buy Wal-Mart's entire stock of chocolate chip cookies. We'll tell citizens over the radio and TV to avoid Main Street after sundown. We'll say we're having anti-terrorist drills."

Although 15,784 chocolate chip cookies were used to set up trails leading to a six-foot high mound of cookies, the zombie didn't show up. It ate two dozen at the beginning of a trail, got full, then disappeared.

The next night, Officer Crouch sat in a gorilla cage on Main Street, wearing a Marilyn Monroe mask and nightgown. She munched chocolate chip cookies, while a hundred cops with fishnets hid in the shadows.

Midnight. All was silent.

"Where's the hell's the zombie?" the Mayor whispered to the Chief.

"Maybe he don't know Marilyn Monroe's waiting for him. Maybe he's prowling some other neighborhood. I think she oughta make woman noises to attract his attention."

"What kinda noises?"

"Maybe she oughta moan like she has a headache, or make believe she's nagging somebody. Or maybe she oughta call out to the zombie. Wait, I got an idea. She can sing *Happy Birthday Mr. President* real loud."

"Hey, Officer Crouch," the Chief said over the radio. "Sing *Happy Birthday Mr. President* like Marilyn Monroe did for President Kennedy. Make it lusty. Better yet, make it sound like you want your head torn off and eaten."

Crouch sang off-key in a screechy voice. After five choruses, an eerie sound could be heard echoing down Main Street. Someone was walking slowly, dragging one foot along the asphalt.

"I see something," the Chief said. "Get ready everybody."

Tension mounted as the zombie reached the cage. Suddenly, it broke out into song, joining Officer Crouch's rendition of *Happy Birthday Mr. President*. Its voice was unbelievably magnificent.

"I'm gonna count to three," the Chief whispered over his radio. "On three, we'll rush him."

"Wait," said the Mayor. "Listen to that voice. He sings better than Pavarotti. It's so fabulous, I can't believe a zombie's singing. Don't capture it until it stops. I don't want voters to think I don't support the arts."

The zombie finished the birthday song, then immediately went into *When Irish Eyes are Smiling.* Next, it sang some old Frank Sinatra tunes. The singing was so beautiful, the cops and Mayor were mesmerized.

When the zombie switched to soft lullabies, all his would-be captors got so relaxed they fell asleep. Snores could be heard from all directions, including the interior of the gorilla cage.

That's when the zombie broke through the bars, tore Marilyn Monroe's head off, and ate it.

Here are some questions about the story:

Was it a complete story?
Did it meet minimalist objectives?
Was it plot-driven?
Was it a fast read?
Was it clearly written?
Was it free of details that weren't vital to the plot?
Did the absence of Mayor's name impact the plot?
Did anything throw you out of the story?
Did you notice emphasis on telling?
Did you learn about the characters through dialog?
Did the story have a protagonist with a goal?
Did the story have an antagonist?

Now that you've seen a flash tale that was written the minimalist way, we'll show it again. This time we've added comments to tell you some of the various minimalist techniques we implemented.

A GOOD FEED

"Chief Carter, I want answers and I want them now! Who's tearing the heads off our beautiful female citizens and eating them?" asked the Mayor.

COMMENTS: Notice how these tightly written sentences work to grab your interest. They also set up the story very quickly. We used only 26 words to do this, so we had plenty left to tell the rest of the story.

Notice the absence of trivial details in the sentences. We omitted the first name of the Chief and the first and last names of Mayor, because we considered them trivial. We're not as concerned about their names as we are the events in which they play a part. In a plot-driven story, events take precedence. We also omitted details about their appearance and what they wore, because none of that mattered to the plot. However, as you proceed, you'll find we mentioned two things that Miss Crouch wore as she sat in the gorilla cage on Main Street. We considered those details vital to the plot.

"I think it's a zombie."

COMMENTS: This line of dialog is as tight as we can make it. Here's an example of how it could've looked if we added more words: "I think it might be a zombie." Or even, "Something tells me it's a zombie." Both sentences would have meant the same as "I think it's a zombie." But the minimalist approach leads us to present the dialog in as few words as possible.

"That's nuts. Werewolves, vampires—those I can understand. But zombies? That's stretching it."

"I sent the killer's MO to police agencies worldwide," said Carter.

COMMENTS: Here's another example of tightly written dialog. He could've said, "Me and my men have spent hundreds of hours checking every police agency in the world." That's a perfectly fine sentence. But from the minimalist point of view, it can be said more briefly. As a minimalist, you'll find yourself rewriting perfectly good sentences that might already be tightly written, to get the idea across in as few words as possible.

"The only answer I got was from Dr. Dumont, Head of the Haitian Zombie Institute. He said a zombie escaped from their research lab a month ago. A vicious monster that feeds on the heads of pretty women. And get this: it likes chocolate chip cookies."

"Sounds bizarre," said the Mayor. "How could a zombie get here from Haiti?"

"Maybe it got to Mexico, then paid a coyote to sneak it across the border."

"What if the missing zombie's the culprit? How can we stop it?"

"Set a trap," said the Chief. I'd like to use your wife as bait."

"Are you crazy?"

COMMENTS: The tight, minimal dialog continues. Notice how it contributes to a fast read. Also note that nothing has been included to interrupt the forward movement of the story. FF should at all times move forward as quickly as possible. Anything less, by definition, means the work really isn't a true genre FF tale. Word count isn't the full measure of what comprises a FF tale.

"She's the best looking woman in town. We can use her to lure the thing. Then my men will jump it with nets."

"No way! I don't want a zombie attacking my wife."

"He won't get near her. We'll put her in a gorilla cage on Main Street. She'll be real safe. Even King Kong couldn't break those bars. My men will hide in the shadows. When we catch the thing, I'll give you the pleasure of killing it—after the news conference where you'll make it sound like you captured it all by yourself. That'll ensure your reelection."

"I doubt my wife would do it. And how do you kill a zombie?"

"With a chain saw."

"Aw, hell. I can't stand the sight of blood."

"Don't worry, Mayor. Dumont said this zombie doesn't have any blood. It's filled with green gunk. The worst that can happen is that you'll get green zombie crud all over your clothes. Ain't that worth reelection?"

"Yeah. But let's keep my wife out of this. Hey, what about using that kid we crowned Miss Pumpkin Festival? She'd make perfect zombie bait."

COMMENTS: We never wasted words describing what any of the characters were wearing, or what they were doing with various body parts during the discussion. For example, we didn't say this: "Aw, hell. I can't stand the sight of blood," the Mayor said, as his jaws tightened. Reports of what happened to his jaw, or eyes, or hands during dialog are trivial, and not vital information for the plot. The story gets along very well without them. The story isn't about what people where doing while they spoke. It's a story about murders and how the authorities will resolve the problem.

"She ain't eighteen yet. Using her could cause big legal headaches for the city."

"Well, who can we get? Who's good looking and brave enough to sit inside a cage in the middle of the night, waiting to be attacked by a zombie?"

"Officer Crouch ain't scared of nothing. Offer her a promotion, and I'll bet she'll volunteer."

"But she looks like she was French kissed by a bulldozer," said the Mayor. "If I was a woman-eating zombie and saw her, I'd lose my appetite and run all the way back to Haiti."

"We could put a Marilyn Monroe mask on her."

"Wouldn't the zombie know and look for somebody else?"

"Not if she's in a cage at night under dim streetlights."

"Hmm," the Mayor said. "Sounds like it might work. On the other hand, you said it likes chocolate chip cookies. Why don't we forget the caged woman idea and buy a bunch of cookies. We can put one every couple of feet to form trails leading to a humongous cookie pile on Main Street. When the zombie reaches the pile, your men could jump it."

"Good idea, Mayor. I'll send somebody to buy Wal-Mart's entire stock of chocolate chip cookies. We'll tell citizens over the radio and TV to avoid Main Street after sundown. We'll say we're having anti-terrorist drills."

Although 15,784 chocolate chip cookies were used to set up trails leading to a six-foot high mound of cookies, the zombie didn't show up. It ate two dozen at the beginning of a trail, got full, then disappeared.

COMMENTS: Notice the quick transition from the idea of buying cookies at Wal-Mart to the fact that cookies were used to trap the zombie. We could've included a sentence or two that said the police went to the store and bought the cookies. We could've said they jumped in their cars and headed to Wal-mart. By omitting details about shopping, nothing is lost. Since this scene shows they now have the cookies, flash readers will assume somebody went to a store and bought them. Thus, we didn't expend precious word count on a scene in which the cookies were purchased. On the other hand, if we decided to reach other publishing markets for this story, such as short story magazines, we'd probably add a scene that tells of the cookie purchase. The only reason for doing that is to expand word count beyond 1,000 words to meet the minimum requirements of a short story.

At times, we've expanded FF tales to convert them to short stories. When doing so, we continued using minimalist techniques to pack even more story telling into the short story versions.

We also write several versions of the same story when we come up with intriguing concepts. This includes changing dialog, characters, and plot variations. We pick the best version for submission to magazines, anthologies, and contests.

The next night, Officer Crouch sat in a gorilla cage on Main Street, wearing a Marilyn Monroe mask and nightgown. She munched chocolate chip cookies, while a hundred cops with fishnets hid in the shadows.

COMMENTS: Another quick transition. Someone who doesn't use minimalist techniques might've told us how she got there, what happened when she went into the cage, what she said, and what else she did besides munch cookies. If we were to write a short story version of this tale, perhaps we might include those details to increase word count. However, the details we'd add would always be related to the plot. And we'd continue to keep the story as lean and as fast-paced as possible.

Midnight. All was silent.

COMMENTS: Notice how we described in so few words what the time was, and the lack of noise. We could've done this a variety of ways, but all would have used more words. These few words help to create an atmosphere, and hopefully raise tension. As you see, there's a place for 1-

word sentence fragments and very short sentences in FF. Short sentences tend to increase tension.

"Where's the hell's the zombie?" the Mayor whispered to the Chief.

"Maybe he don't know Marilyn Monroe's waiting for him. Maybe he's prowling some other neighborhood. I think she oughta make woman noises to attract his attention."

"What kinda noises?"

"Maybe she oughta moan like she has a headache, or make believe she's nagging somebody. Or maybe she oughta call out to the zombie. Wait, I got an idea. She can sing *Happy Birthday Mr. President* real loud."

"Hey, Officer Crouch," the Chief said over the radio. "Sing *Happy Birthday Mr. President* like Marilyn Monroe did for President Kennedy. Make it lusty. Better yet, make it sound like you want your head torn off and eaten."

Crouch sang off-key in a screechy voice. After five choruses, an eerie sound could be heard echoing down Main Street. Someone was walking slowly, dragging one foot along the asphalt.

"I see something," the Chief said. "Get ready, everybody."

Tension mounted as the zombie reached the cage. Suddenly, it broke out into song, joining Officer Crouch's rendition of *Happy Birthday Mr. President*. Its voice was unbelievably magnificent.

COMMENTS: Notice how quickly we got the zombie to the cage. Note also that we didn't bother to describe him. Flash readers already have a picture of zombies in their imaginations. No need to waste words giving them such details. That might've slowed down the story. At this point, the story isn't about what he wore, it's about his capture.

We also told readers that tension mounted. This points out a significant difference between FF and short stories and novels. The other storytelling methods would show us how tension mounted among the characters in various ways. That could take dozens of words.

We took a risk in using Happy Birthday Mr. President, because the song came from an incident well-covered on TV during John F. Kennedy's presidency. Many younger readers, especially from other countries, may not know about this, or appreciate the significance of that event.

"I'm gonna count to three," the Chief whispered over his radio. "On three, we'll rush him."

"Wait," said the Mayor. "Listen to that voice. He sings better than Pavarotti. It's so fabulous, I can't believe a zombie's singing. Don't capture it until it stops. I don't want voters to think I don't support the arts."

The zombie finished the birthday song, then immediately went into *When Irish Eyes are Smiling.* Next, it sang some old Frank Sinatra tunes. The singing was so beautiful, the cops and Mayor were mesmerized.

When the zombie switched to soft lullabies, all his would-be captors got so relaxed they fell asleep. Snores could be heard from all directions, including the interior of the gorilla cage.

That's when the zombie broke through the bars, tore Marilyn Monroe's head off, and ate it.

COMMENTS: We used contractions 37 times in this story to trim word count. Candidates for contractions are word-wasters, such as I am, she is, they are, and so on. Each time they appear, 1 word is wasted. Converting them to contractions saves 1 word each time. Consequently, we cut the story's length by 37 words by replacing word-wasters with contractions.

Here are the all contractions that appear in the story: *who's, it's, that's, I'd, don't, won't, we'll, she'll, couldn't, I'll, you'll, that'll, that's, I'm, hell's, wouldn't, she's, he's, can't, doesn't, let's, she'd.*

Remember, the objectives of the minimalist way are to tell as much story as possible in as few words as possible, without sacrificing a smooth read. Using contractions helps meet these objectives.

Contractions also make the dialog sound more natural, and they help to move the story forward more quickly.

Perhaps you noticed this story contains 3 scenes:

- The discussion between the Chief and Mayor

- The first attempt to capture the zombie using cookies

- The second attempt to capture the zombie

We've found 3 to 4 scenes are ideal for FF. We've seen some instances of 5, but we felt the extra scene was added at the expense of developing other scenes more fully.

We've seen a FF story with ten scenes. Most were underdeveloped, making the read choppy. The author tried to tell too much in 1,000 words. That was an instance in which a story idea wasn't a good candidate for the FF format.

Q24: What's the ideal number of scenes of a FF tale?

The zombie story has 4 major characters: the Chief, Mayor, Crouch, and the zombie. We think this is the maximum for any FF story; otherwise, the story becomes difficult to follow.

Q25: What's the ideal number of characters for a FF story?

Here's a summary of what we covered in this lesson:

- Overview of the genre FF development process.

- Tips for naming characters the minimalist way.

- Counting words in a FF tale.

- Tips when reading your first draft.

- Example of a prize-winning FF tale developed the minimalist way.

- How minimalist approach techniques were applied to the sample story.

- Ideal number of scenes in a FF tale.

- Ideal number of characters in a FF tale.

This concludes Lesson-2.

LESSON-3

WRITING OPENING SENTENCES THE MINIMALIST WAY

This lesson covers the following:

- Opening sentences that hook

- Sentences that don't hook

- Problems when devising opening sentences

- How words are wasted in opening sentences

WRITING OPENING SENTENCES THAT HOOK

The ideal way to open a flash tale is to include a sentence that hooks readers. This technique is not unique to the minimalist way of story development. You've probably heard the advantages of writing opening sentences that hook ever since high school. It becomes more important than ever when it comes to flash. The idea is to engage readers as quickly as possible.

Which of the thirty opening sentences shown below grab your attention and make you want to read more? Ask yourself why it hooked you.

- *Sarah Brown lived in a house that had ten windows and a flat roof.*

- *The Martian sat placidly on a park bench and wondered why Earth's sky was blue.*

- *I wanted to write a long poem about flowers, so I got my pen and notebook.*

- *Bill decided to kill the first woman he saw with red hair.*

- *Aunt Polly finished her breakfast of toast and coffee.*

- *Mary thought it a good day to make a new dress, so she went to the closet that was wallpapered with sunflowers and grabbed the sewing machine—the one her good friend Lucy gave her as a birthday present.*

- *When Billy woke up and saw snow, he decided to make a snowman.*

- *"Aunt Edna, why are you sticking a long needle in that doll's eye, and saying those funny words?"*

- *While riding my bicycle, I crashed right into a four-eyed, orange alien.*

- *Harry decided to take a nap in the new hammock he just bought.*

- *Judy didn't believe in zombies until she arrived in Haiti.*

- *Mary's hair refused to cooperate.*

- *"Shoot the bastard before he strangles you!" Harry yelled.*

- *The door opened to reveal the most beautiful hunk of woman this side of the Mississippi.*

- *"Where can I get this candy recipe?" asked Lisa.*

- *Wilma turned on the TV to catch the President's latest speech about the need to declare World War Ten on the Eskimos.*

- *The moment Charlie touched the door handle, he noticed a blue fungus growing on the door.*

- *"I'm out of ammunition!" Bill yelled as hordes of crazed pink rabbits charged up the hill.*

- *When I first met Harriet, my heart almost burst through my chest.*

- *"How many sandwiches do you think we'll need for the picnic?" asked Aunty Em.*

- *I dialed 911 the moment I saw the pregnant woman trip on the pavement.*

- *"This is the best book I've ever read," Wanda said to Mary, after she dropped another sugar cube into her steaming coffee.*

- *The bus hit Frank, dragging him a hundred feet.*

- *When Charles opened the door to the old house, his hair stood straight up.*

- *While Miriam rinsed her hair in the shower, the lights went out.*

- *My dog went crazy when he saw the cat.*

- *"Swing the bat harder," yelled the coach.*

- *"Please save me from the monster," the woman hollered as they strapped her to the hospital bed.*

- *When Sgt. Giddings stepped forward, a landmine exploded.*

- *Charlie sank into the chair by the fireplace.*

Now that you've seen some grabbers and yawners, here are some we wrote for stories that got published in magazines and anthologies. Two were openers for stories that won first prize in writing contests. The story title appears first, then the opening sentence. See if they grab you enough to make you want to read more.

MOON COOKIES: *Billy was in grandma's kitchen when his thumb fell off.*

ROUTE 22: *"I wouldn't risk taking Route 22 back to Phoenix tonight, I were you," the bartender said.*

$39.50 A PLATE: *Billions were petrified when Mars was larger than the full Moon in the night sky.*

SEARCHING FOR DR. HARLOW: *My best friend, Dr. Rolf Harlow, disappeared while searching for zombies in Haiti.*

RED DUST: *The priest sensed a profound change of atmosphere the moment someone entered the darkened confessional.* (This story won first prize in a writing contest.)

RAH-RAH-SHISH-BOOM-SNAKE: *The sound of drums was manic, horrific.* (This story won first prize in a writing contest.)

A CHUNK OF CONCRETE: *From dusk to dawn, Harry rode the New York subway seeking foul things that prowled the night.*

WILMA'S PASSION: *"Step right up, ladies and gentlemen," yelled the carnival barker, "and see Herbie, the friendliest zombie in the world."*

M: *When Martian hordes invaded, we fled to the forest.*

THE PINK CONTRACT: *"Mister, would you like to buy some nice dreams?"*

A BIG WAD OF CASH: *Charlie's mom was convinced werewolves were roaming the woods near her house.*

HIGHWAY 35: *The cop vomited when he turned on his flashlight and looked inside the Lexus.*

THE GOLDEN GODDESS: *Weird things began to happen after Sam stole the gold statue of the Smiling Chinese Goddess.*

Notice how these opening sentences bring you into the story very quickly. Let's take the one from *Highway 35* as an example. *The cop vomited when he turned on his flashlight and looked inside the Lexus.* An editor who reads this might wonder why that happened and want to read more.

Writing a snappy opening sentence to entice editors is always a challenge. However, when you create one, you face the additional challenge of developing a tale that sustains editor's interest through to the end.

Let's look again at the first sentence from our 950-word flash tale, *Moon Cookies: Billy was in Grandma's kitchen when his thumb fell off.*

- How did you react when reading this sentence?

- What questions came to your mind after reading about Billy's finger?

Write an opening sentence for a new story that has a hook. Ask someone to read it. Then ask the reader if it grabbed his or her attention.

Here's another of our opening sentences from a published story: *Liz shuddered, as Dr. Zangara approached her with a huge syringe filled with murky yellow fluid.* Suppose you'd written this. What would you write in the next sentence?

HOW WORDS ARE WASTED IN OPENING SENTENCES

Now that we showed you some openers that worked, here are some that didn't. Let's examine them closely so you don't make the same mistakes. Here's the first one:

"What have you done?" Jane demanded, precociously imperious at nine years old.

Here's why this sentence contains wasted words:

- *Nine years old* is a trivial detail that isn't vital to the plot. We know that from reading the story.

- *Precociously imperious* is another trivial detail.

The words *precociously imperious are* an example of pompous prose that could throw readers out of the story while they pause to consult a dictionary.

When pompous prose occurs in flash, we suspect the author's trying to impress readers with his literary sophistication and ability to string fancy words together. But all this does is plug two needless words into the story. Needless words are always wasted words. Which leads us to an important point to consider: always use simple words in minimalist FF.

Something else struck us in this example: *demanded.* The word *asked* would've sufficed. Many magazine editors prefer authors to stick with *asked* and *said*, instead of going through syntactical gymnastics trying to find substitutes. This subject is covered more thoroughly in Lesson-5.

Actually, the opening sentence would work better, if *demanded* is changed to *asked*, and everything beyond that is deleted. Rewritten it'd look like this: *"What have you done?" Jane asked.*

Q26: What potential problem occurs when readers encounter pompous prose in the opening sentence?

Q27: Here's a 16-word long opening sentence: *In a red beret with a black woolen scarf, she walks up to the candy counter.* What trivial details appear in this opening sentence?

Q28: How many words can you save by deleting all the wasted ones?

By the way, the sentence about the woman with the red beret was written in present tense. We suggest you avoid present tense, because it limits your ability to tell the story to its fullest potential. In the hundreds of magazine submission guidelines we've read, many say they don't accept stories in present tense.

Maybe talking about what somebody wore in the opening sentence would work if you said something like this: *Harry put on a bulletproof vest and charged into the bank.*

Look at the difference if the sentence was written like this: *Harry put on a brand new, dark blue Kevlar bulletproof vest, which he'd never worn before, and charged into the bank.*

Now the sentence is loaded trivial details. The color of the vest or its age aren't vital to the story. Same goes for the idea that he'd never worn it before.

Notice how unwieldy opening sentences can be when they're taken to extremes. This one's 31 words long: *The family stood looking down at the hospital bed, in which the blue and gray tubes and clear plastic bags seemed to form a cocoon or a web, overwhelming the patient.*

Notice also how the author wasted words giving us a choice of how to visualize the plastic bags, comparing them to *a cocoon*, or *a web*. Seems the author wasn't too sure what the scene should look like to his characters.

Q29: Reduce the 31-word sentence above to the fewest words possible.

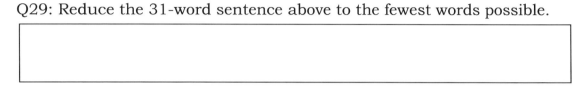

Let's look at another kind of error we've often seen in opening sentences. In this one, the author provided a neat opening sentence that hooked us, but the very next sentence changed the subject. This caused us to lose interest immediately.

Opening Sentence: *Fish were feeding on our eyelids, and I couldn't make them stop.*

Second Sentence: *It was 115 degrees, and I was standing watch on the door gun just before our chopper crashed.*

The idea of fish feeding on somebody's eyelids is a grabber. We couldn't wait to read more about this macabre situation. To our dismay, the writer changed the subject by giving a weather report and telling us the protagonist stood watch before a helicopter crashed.

This is a major weakness in the story's structure. As magazine editors, we rejected stories that did this. We got the impression authors thought they only needed to hook us with a great opening sentence, and we'd automatically accept their work. We reminded them in rejection letters that they had to sustain our interest throughout the entire piece.

Don't fall into that trap. If you create an opening sentence that can knock the socks off your readers, don't do anything in the next sentence to ruin the effect.

Here's another example:

Opening Sentence: *When my wife came back she was different.*

Second Sentence: *All night when I lay beside her, I'd only pretend to sleep.*

The first sentence intrigued us. We wanted to know how she was different. We hoped she'd been abducted and had returned as some kind of monster. Unfortunately, the very next sentence changed the subject and told us about a guy in bed. We never found out what was different about her, nor where she'd gone.

The minimalist approach to writing opening sentences means we will use the fewest words possible to grab the reader's attention. At the same time, we will try to thrust the reader right into the story. If done right, the opening sentence serves as an effective set up.

Here's one that violates the minimalist approach by containing 27 words: *Melvin Smith's face flushed with excitement, and his sweaty hands twisted and turned atop the smooth mahogany desk that loomed in front of him like an ocean.* Notice how it's loaded with trivial details that can't possibly be vital to the plot.

Q30: List the trivial details in this sentence: *Melvin Smith's face flushed with excitement, and his sweaty hands twisted and turned atop the smooth mahogany desk that loomed in front of him like an ocean.*

Q31: What are the main ideas buried in this sentence? *Melvin Smith's face flushed with excitement, and his sweaty hands twisted and turned atop the smooth mahogany desk that loomed in front of him like an ocean.*

Q32: Considering the ideas you've culled from the sentence, rewrite it in as few words as possible to meet minimalist objectives. Hint: we did it in 9 words. We omitted his last name, because last names are wasted words in FF, unless the character is famous.

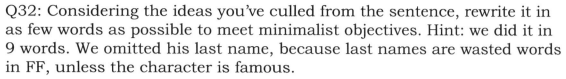

Another thing to omit in opening sentences is weather reports. We've critiqued hundreds of flash tales that started this way. In each instance, weather had nothing to do with the plot. It was merely a superfluous filler.

One story included a weather report set in October, complete with candy wrappers and old newspapers being tossed about the streets by brisk winds. As it turned out, the story was about rampaging zombies, which had nothing to do with the weather. It might've been important if the zombies restricted their attacks only on windy days in October when candy wrappers and newspapers were blowing through the streets.

The writer missed an opportunity to give a zippy opener to thrust us right into a zombie attack. But that was delayed and didn't show up until much later in the story. Before we reached the fun parts, we had to wade through paragraphs of trivial details and unnecessary descriptions that only slowed the read and got us yawning. Don't make these kinds of mistakes in your stories, no matter what genre you're writing.

We also noticed that all stories opening with weather reports suddenly changed the subject in the next sentence. Then the weather wasn't mentioned again. We wondered why it was there in the first place.

Here's an example from a crime tale: *It wasn't always raining in Portland, but when the sun did come out you didn't really notice it until it was gone again.* As expected, the next sentence changed the subject by mentioning a crime victim. The weather was never mentioned again. We wondered why the author didn't write an opening sentence about the victim.

If you find it necessary to open with a weather report, ensure it's vital to the plot. An example is when the story is about nuclear winter with radioactive snowfall, after an atomic explosion. Another is an incident that occurs during a tornado, when the tornado plays a key role in the story. Perhaps you can think of other instances in which weather should be mentioned in the opening sentence. However, in the thousands of stories we've critiqued, we've never run across one that needed to begin with a weather report.

Here's an opener that's quite dense and includes alliteration. *Scream shattered silence jerked Jim awake.* This serves as a good example of muddled writing that threw us out of the story. No matter how many times we read this, we couldn't figure out what the author was saying.

Here's a summary of what we covered in this lesson:

- Opening sentences that hook.

- Sentences that fail to hook.

- Hooking readers, then changing the subject.

- Avoiding long opening sentences.

- Why weather reports are superfluous openers.

This concludes Lesson-3.

LESSON-4

WRITING DIALOG THE MINIMALST WAY

This lesson covers the following:

- Reasons for including dialog.
- Writing dialog the minimalist way.
- Converting narrative to dialog.
- Example of prize-winning story consisting entirely of dialog.
- Reasons for including some substandard English.

REASONS FOR INCLUDING DIALOG

Include dialog to make FF tales more exciting and dramatic. Well-crafted dialog usually takes fewer words than narrative. To illustrate this, let's look at the opening of a fantasy tale that consists only of narrative. Then we'll show you the same opener converted to dialog. We've used our published story, "A Few Abnormalities," to illustrate the differences. For greater impact, we suggest you read both versions out loud.

NARRATIVE VERSION:

She called and said she was a mermaid. I figured she was nuts. I told her I was Spiderman just to be facetious. I told her I figured she was a telemarketer who'd say anything just to keep me on the phone. When I said that, she claimed she never heard the word telemarketer and didn't know what it meant. Then I asked why she called. She said she wanted to hear my voice. Her voice wasn't familiar, so I asked who she was. She told me her name. It was very long. She said she didn't expect me to remember her, although in the past, I'd whispered her name so many times. She claimed she'd comforted me in her arms the awful night I was delirious. She said she gave me warmth and tenderness. Then her voice broke, and she said she'd given me all the love within her being.

DIALOG VERSION:

"Did you say you're a mermaid?"

"Yes," said the female voice.

"And I'm Spiderman," I said. "I swear, you telemarketers will say anything to keep people on the phone."

"Telemarketers? I don't know that word."

"Then why'd you call?"

"To hear your voice."

"Who is this?" I asked.

"Shantakumari. I don't expect you to remember me. But you whispered my name many times, so long ago. When I comforted you in my arms during that awful night you were delirious. I gave you warmth, tenderness." Her voice broke. "And I gave you all the love within my being."

The narrative version of this fantasy scene has 153 words, while the dialog version has 98. That's a 55 word difference.

Here's another situation in which switching to dialog reduced word count. We'll show you both versions so you can compare them.

NARRATIVE: *Martha was holding a red can. I asked her what it was for.*

DIALOG: *"Martha, what's that red can for?" I asked.*

The narrative contains 13 words, the dialog contains 8.

Q33: From the minimalist viewpoint, what's an advantage of converting narrative to dialog?

_____

Here's another example:

NARRATIVE: *Whispering, she asked him for a kiss.*

DIALOG: *"Kiss me," she whispered.*

Notice the effect we get by changing narrative to dialog. Read both versions aloud and consider which is more dramatic. Do this with your own work when you're trying to decide which has more punch.

Q34: Consider this sentence: *Jason wanted to kiss her, but she refused.* Convert this to dialog. Make her refusal sound angry. Use as few words as possible. Hint: There are several ways to convert this into dialog.

Q35: This example is for a horror tale. *Somebody saw a monster. Harold suggested they run away.* Change this to dialog, using as few words as possible. Hint: There are many ways to do this.

Here's an example where adding dialog to create tension uses more words than the narrative. In this scene, 4 women in an isolated place find all the tires slashed on their car. Here's the narrative: *The four women stood looking at the tires, then back at one another, unable to speak.* This sentence doesn't create drama or tension. When converting to dialog for this lesson, we decided the 4 characters should do more than look at each other and remain silent.

> *"Look at my tires!" Anna yelled. "They're all flat!"*
> *"They were slashed." Barb said, pointing to deep cuts.*
> *"I'm scared," said Clara. "It's getting dark."*
> *"Stay close to me," Donna said, pulling a pistol from her purse.*

We decided to create some fear and tension, and to include a pistol, though none of these appeared in the narrative. By doing so, we *increased* word count by 21 words. This is the opposite of our minimalist objectives. However, we thought the changes justified the increased word count. To make up for expending extra words, we examined the student's manuscript very closely and found places where we could tighten sentences and delete 21 words.

We've never seen a flash tale in which we couldn't reduce word count, then apply the gained words to better advantage somewhere else in the story.

WRITING DIALOG THE MINIMALIST WAY

The minimalist approach to writing dialog is to keep it as concise and crisp as possible without sacrificing a smooth read.

Here's an example of an all-dialog, 497-word FF tale we wrote for a contest. Guidelines allowed us to include *he said* or *she said* only 3 times. Our submission won first prize.

Here's the story. As you read it, see if we accomplished our minimalist objectives.

TELL YOU WHAT I'M GONNA DO

"Hey, Kid, give it a try. Ten chances for a dollar. Toss a ping-pong ball in the basket. If it stays in, you win the best prizes on the Midway."

"But your shelves are empty. Where are the prizes?"

"In your head."

"Whadda ya mean?"

"If you win, you get whatever you want. Name it, and you got it. But you gotta tell me within one second after the ball settles in the basket. If you take longer, you lose."

"I bet if I win and say Mustang convertible, you'll give me a little toy car."

"No way. See all those trailers parked over there? They're loaded with prizes. New cars. Designer clothes. Gold jewelry. Anything a teenager like you could ever want. You name it, I got it."

"You're kidding."

"Nope. See that gal in the tight red jeans at the hot dog stand? She won a solid-gold watch a few minutes ago. Ask her to show it to you."

"Excuse me, Lady. The guy over there said you won a gold watch from him. Is that true?"

"Yep. Look at this beauty. I'll bet it's worth ten thousand bucks. I won it on my eighth try."

"Wow! I'm gonna go back there and see if I can win a car."

"Good luck," she said.

"I see you're back. How many balls do you want?"

"Ten."

"Here you go. Good luck."

"Hey! I won!"

"Forfeit," he said. "You didn't name your prize within a second."

"Aw hell. Well, watch closely, because I'm gonna win again. Yahoo! BUBBLE GUM."

"We got a winaaaa! Here's a piece of bubble gum, Kid. Chew it in good health."

"Wait. Something weird just happened. I was gonna say Mustang convertible, but somehow I ended up saying bubble gum. That sure as hell ain't gonna happen again. Gimme ten more balls."

"Here you go. Good luck. Hey, don't lean over the counter like that. It's against the rules."

"Sorry. Okay...watch this. PLASTIC COMB."

"We got a winaaaa! You're a very lucky kid. Here's a nice comb for your curly hair."

"Dammit! It happened again. I don't know why I said plastic comb instead of Mustang convertible."

"You must be over excited. Tell you what I'm gonna do. Next time you win, I'll name the prize for you."

"Really?"

"I swear. What color convertible do you want?"

"Candy apple red."

"Okay, Kid. Win again, and I'll name it for you."

"Damn! I can't seem to get any balls in the basket."

"Maybe you'll get lucky with the next one."

"Hey! I won!

"Your immortal soul," he said

"What? You were supposta say Mustang convertible."

"Sorry. My mistake. Tell you what I'm gonna do. Whadda ya say we make a trade. I'll give you a Mustang convertible right now for your immortal soul."

"What's that?"

"Nothing compared to a beautiful new car. Think of all the hot chicks you'll be able to pickup. Is it a deal?"

"Hell yeah."

"We got another winaaaa!"

End

Here are some questions about the story:

> Was it a complete story?
> Did it meet minimalist objectives?
> Was it plot-driven?
> Was it a fast read?
> Was it clearly written?
> Was it free of details that weren't vital to the plot?
> Did the absence of Kid's name impact the plot?
> Did the absence of barker's name impact the plot?
> Did anything throw you out of the story?
> Did you notice emphasis on telling?
> Did you learn about the characters through dialog?
> Did the story have a protagonist with a goal?
> Did the story have an antagonist?

The piece you just read included 10 instances of substandard English, including *whadda, gonna, supposta, hafta,* and others. We included them, to save 1 word each time, for a total of 10. These also make the dialog more realistic as people rarely speak in formal English.

Don't be reluctant to use words like this in FF. We've never received a rejection for including them.

The story also includes 16 contractions, such as *I'm, you'll, I'll,* and others. Including them saved 16 more words. Thus, we trimmed a total of 26 words. If we hadn't used these word-count saving devices, the story would've exceeded the 500 words allowed by the contest guidelines.

There are lots of pitfalls to avoid when writing FF dialog. Most involve word-wasters. The next lesson identifies ten kinds and shows how to deal with them.

Here's a summary of what we covered in this lesson:

- Reasons for including dialog.
- Writing dialog the minimalist way.
- Converting narrative to dialog.
- Example of a prize-winning story consisting entirely of dialog.
- Reasons for using some substandard English.

This concludes Lesson-4

LESSON-5

WORD-WASTERS IN DIALOG

This lesson identifies 10 kinds of word-wasters to omit from FF dialog:

- Action tags.
- Words that can be converted to contractions.
- Repetition.
- Unnecessary interruptions.
- Slang.
- Foreign words.
- Regional dialects.
- Idiomatic expressions.
- Said bookisms.
- Descriptions of how characters speak.

Q36: Name at least 6 word-wasters to omit when creating dialog. If you can't, go back and read the list again.

Let's take a closer look at them...

ACTION TAGS

To understand the function of action tags in a sentence, look at the illustration below, which includes the sentence: "I'm sorry," she said, wringing her hands, and sighing.

DIALOG	DIALOG TAG	ACTION TAG
"I'm sorry,"	she said,	wringing her hands and sighing.

Action tags account for the largest amount of wasted words we find in FF tales. Authors use them to describe every possible bodily movement known to mankind, no matter how minute, such as:

- Blinking
- Leaning
- Nodding
- Raising
- Rolling
- Scratching
- Shifting
- Shrugging
- Sighing
- Sniffing
- Turning
- Twisting

Novels and short stories are usually loaded with trivial action tags. We're told in creative writing courses and how-to books that including them aids in character development. Since genre FF doesn't focus on character-development, minimalists should omit trivial action tags. Here's why:

- They burn up lots of word count.
- They slow down the read.
- They can stall the read.
- They can be distracting, because they often intrude and draw attention to themselves.

- They always contain trivial details that can get boring very quickly.
- They don't add anything of value to the plot.

Q37: Name at least 3 reasons we gave you for avoiding trivial action tags from dialog:

When we encounter a FF tale loaded with trivial action tags—and many include them after every line of dialog—we know immediately the story has little or zero plot. We urge you not to approach genre FF as if it's nothing more than a mini-novel.

Here's an example of a conversation that's loaded with trivial action tags:

"Are you enjoying your lunch?" Harry asked, as he shifted in his chair.
"Yes. "My salami sandwich is delicious," Mary said," as she bit into the sour dough bread that had arrived from San Francisco in a blue truck that very morning. "What about your liverwurst sandwich? Is it worth the price?" She shooed a fly from her nose, as her gaze fell upon a placard that advertised pie for only fifteen cents a slice.
Scratching his cheek, Harry thought for a few moments before answering. Screwing up his face, he said, "I've had better."

This scene contains 95 words. 30 were expended on dialog and tags. The remaining 65—which accounts for 68% of the scene's word count—were wasted on trivial details via action tags. This includes:

- Shooing flies
- Shifting in a chair
- The kind of bread
- Where it came from
- How it got there
- The color of the vehicle that delivered it
- The time of day it arrived

- Face scratching
- Gazing on a placard
- What a character's face was doing

This raises a question: how can shooing flies during a discussion between two characters be relevant in any way to the plot of a genre FF tale? It isn't, unless the plot's about a fly invasion. So far, we haven't run across any fly-invasion plots in thousands of stories. Nevertheless, we continue to read FF stories that include shooing flies and endless reports of shrugging, raising eyebrows, turning, and hundreds of others body movements.

After reading over 6,000 stories loaded with trivial action tags, we've formulated Minimalist Rule #1 for Flash Fiction: Excessive trivial details = little or zero plot. We've never seen this rule disproven.

Here's the same scene with action tags and what happens when we remove them:

WITH ACTION TAGS	NO ACTION TAGS
"Are you enjoying your lunch?" Harry asked, as he shifted in his chair. *"Yes," said Mary. "My salami sandwich is delicious," Mary replied, as she bit into the sour dough bread that had arrived from San Francisco in a blue truck that very morning. "What about your liverwurst sandwich? Is it worth the price?" She shooed a fly from her nose, as her gaze fell upon a placard that advertised pie for only fifteen cents a slice.* *Scratching his cheek, Harry thought for a few moments before answering. Screwing up his face, he said, "I've had better."*	*"Are you enjoying your lunch?"Harry asked.* *"Yes. My salami Sandwich is delicious," said Mary. "What about your liverwurst sandwich? Is it worth the price?"* *"I've had better."*

Q38: Rewrite the following two sentences to eliminate wasted words: *Scratching his cheek, Harry thought for a few moments before answering. Screwing up his face, he said, "I've had better."* Hint: try a single sentence.

Q39: How many words did you delete?_____

Q40: Besides wasting words, trivial details have two more detrimental effects on dialog. Name them.

Look at this example: *"Have you heard of the Mysterious Caves?" Karl paused just long enough to watch Helga's expression of curiosity before going on.* If this is supposed to be a fast-moving flash tale, we wonder why a character must pause? And why did the author waste words describing the duration of the pause? From the minimalist viewpoint, this is needless filler.

Deleting trivial action tags from the sentence eliminates 14 words that can be applied elsewhere in the story—especially to create more drama and strengthen the plot.

In this example, we get 2 words of dialog followed by 19 trivial words in an action tag: *"Did he?" She jams her hands into her coat pockets and walks over to him, the old floorboards creaking in protest.* This shows to what extent writers will go to fill FF with needless fluff that does nothing for the story or plot.

Here's another example: *"She's a snob," Jones, a paunchy old man with thick glasses wearing a shrunken, grimy t-shirt said, skulking.*

Q41: Delete trivial details in action tags and rewrite the sentence shown above.

```
                                                                        
                                                                        
                                                                        
                                                                        
```

Q42: How many words did you delete? _____

We don't want to give you the impression that all action tags are trivial. Here's an example of one that's vital to the story: *"Raise your hands, or I'll blow your head off," Charlie yelled, pulling his pistol.*

Action tags can appear in front of dialog. Here's an example: *Derek's mother put down her book and rubbed her eyes. "Of course. It's not a word we use in polite conversation, and it's terribly insulting."*

Once again, we have trivial details in an action tag that do nothing for the plot. The entire tag could have been omitted, saving 10 words and making the read a bit faster.

WORDS THAT CAN BE CONVERTED TO CONTRACTIONS

Convert words to contractions every chance you have when writing dialog. Each instance reduces word count by 1.

For example, if you write this sentence: *I am terribly sorry,* you can save 1 word by changing *I am* to *I'm.* This makes dialog smoother and more natural-sounding.

Here are some examples of contractions:

- *I'm replaces I am.*
- S*he'll* replaces *She will.*
- *It'd* replaces *It would.*
- *We're* replaces *We are.*
- *You're* replaces *You are.*
- *I'd promised Susan I wouldn't gamble.* replaces *I had promised Susan I would not gamble.*
- *"I'm going home."* replaces *"I am going home."*
- *"The Browns'll arrive soon."* replaces *"The Browns will arrive soon."*
- *"He's gonna shoot."* replaces *"He is gonna shoot."*

Q43: Rewrite this sentence by changing whatever you can to contractions. *I will see you when I get there, but you will have to make sure you are on time.*

```
┌─────────────────────────────────────────────────────────────┐
│                                                             │
│                                                             │
│                                                             │
│                                                             │
└─────────────────────────────────────────────────────────────┘
```

Q44: How many contractions are in your rewritten sentence?

_____

REPETITION

Needless repetition is another word-waster in dialog. Here's an example:

"So, he liked to talk?" asked Frank.

"He loved to talk. He loved it," Mary said.

Q45: Rewrite Mary's dialog to conform with minimalist objectives.

```
┌─────────────────────────────────────────────────────────────┐
│                                                             │
│                                                             │
│                                                             │
└─────────────────────────────────────────────────────────────┘
```

Remember: you're in absolute control of what your characters say. As a minimalist, don't let them waste words when they speak. Make their dialog as crisp and concise as possible, and don't let them repeat anything unnecessarily.

Here's another example:

"We better get out of here. The cops are coming."
"Did you say the cops are coming?"
"Yeah, the cops are coming."

Q46: Rewrite the second and third lines of the dialog above to reduce them to the fewest number of words.

```
┌─────────────────────────────────────────────────────────────┐
│                                                             │
│                                                             │
│                                                             │
└─────────────────────────────────────────────────────────────┘
```

Another example: *"Come in, come in young man, you're getting soaked."*

Q47: Delete the repetitious dialog and rewrite: *"I need to get home, I need to get home on the next plane," Lisa said.*

```



```

Here's another form of repetition in dialog: *"That's enough!" Lois cut her off.* Notice how the dialog shows Lois is cutting somebody off. And yet the author reminds us via narrative by telling us Lois is cutting somebody off. This is needless repetition.

Examine this example:

> *Something hit the widow. Bill went to take a look. He returned carrying a half-eaten pancake.*
> *"It's a pancake," Bill said to Lois.*
> *"A pancake?" Lois asked. "Why would somebody hit our window with a pancake?*

Q48: How would you rewrite Lois' dialog to eliminate repetition and reduce word count? HINT: Consider if it's necessary to include *Lois asked.*

```



```

This example stalls the story:

> *"Don't," Lisa simply said.*
> *"What?"*
> *"Don't," she repeated.*
> *"Don't make fun of nutty professors who have gone off the deep end?*

Another example: *"Theresa," she hissed. "It's Theresa."*

This one includes narrative then dialog:

> *The sky was very dark.*
> *"Why, why is it dark? Has it always been this dark? Is it night, or is it day? If so, why so dark?"*
> *Still the sky was dark.*

This example is one of many instances in which the sentences have to be rewritten for word economy. In this case, either the dialog or narrative should mention the sky is very dark only once, then it's time to get the story moving forward.

Remember: when writing dialog, always strive for word economy. That doesn't mean you should cut it down so far that it isn't clear. Use your best judgment.

UNNECESSARY INTERRUPTIONS

This word-waster occurs when authors interrupt a perfectly good dialog stream to tell us something completely unrelated to the conversation. Usually it's done to report an insignificant movement of some body part, and it's never about anything vital to the plot. Here's an example:

> *"If I ever catch you hanging around him again, I'll slash your damn throat!" Bill hollered.*
> *"That's a lot of big talk from a nothing guy like you," said Lisa.*
> *"So now you're going to smart-mouth me on top of everything else. I should smash your face before I slit your throat."*
> *He stared at her, while wiping sweat from his brow. With the other hand, he scratched his ear.*
> *"You try it and you'll be a dead man."*

Notice how the interruption about staring, wiping sweat, and scratching immediately diminishes the tension and drama the author was building so nicely.

WORD-WASTERS THAT THROW READERS OUT OF THE STORY

The following word-wasters in dialog can slow down the story and throw readers out of it:

- Slang
- Foreign words
- Idiomatic expressions
- Regional dialects
- Said bookisms

Let's review them and their detrimental effects on FF dialog...

SLANG

Slang can date your story, making it obsolete. Today's popular slang may disappear tomorrow. It can also be unclear to many readers who may not have heard the expression. It can throw readers out of the story, as they pause to figure out what the words mean.

Slang often uses more words than those it replaces. Here are a few examples:

- *duke it out*
- *whole nother*
- *gross-out*
- *nuke*
- *zone in on*
- *easy mark*
- *cut out*
- *psych out*
- *snow job*
- *deep pockets*
- *knuckle sandwich*
- *couch potato*
- *roach coach*

FOREIGN WORDS

Omit foreign words. Example: *Chasing women was Frank's raison d'etre.* Many genre fiction readers won't know what this means, and it may throw them out of the story. The appearance of foreign words also tends to give readers a sense that the author is trying to convey a high level of sophistication. Here are a few examples of hundreds we've seen in flash tales:

- *mon dieu*
- *coup de grace*
- *je ne sais quoi*
- *kvetch*
- *deux ex machine*
- *savoir-faire*
- *shmultz*
- *voila*
- *carniceria*
- *quid pro quo*
- *schlemiel*

Sometimes we run across dialog from space aliens, such as this example: *"Allanda yuni tushna, tewek thanock?"*

REGIONAL DIALECTS

Omit regional dialects. Some authors think it's necessary to reproduce exactly how characters from various parts of the nation speak. Perhaps that works well in novels and short stories, but not in FF. Not only does it slow the read, as we try to pronounce and decipher what's being said, but it also throws us out of the story. Regional dialect also risks offending readers who think their pronunciation is perfectly proper and don't think it needs to be spelled out.

Here are a few we've seen in stories. We're not sure what regions of the country they represent. However, all of them made us stumble and threw us out of the story. You can imagine how laborious the read becomes when a story contains several paragraphs of this kind of dialect.

- *"This is the spot, i'n' it — where it 'appened. Where I snuffed it. Gowd, 'ow long's it been?"*
- *"I'm going to Korear to furthah my careah."*
- *"Werah y'at?"*
- *"Urt! Yer on yer own, Kiddarooni!"*
- *"Well o' course 'e never listened. Left me, 'e did."*
- *"Never said nuffin bout what Pauley had twixt flesh and bone."*
- *Yinz* = Plural of *you*
- *Noo Yawk* = *New York*
- *Awl bidniz* = oil business
- *Boh-uhl* = bottle

IDIOMATIC EXPRESSIONS

Omit idiomatic expressions whenever possible. They may be unfamiliar to readers, especially when English is their second language. If your work is published in an online magazine, it will be available to readers around the world, so do all you can to accommodate your global audience.

Many English idiomatic expressions burn up too much word count. Example: *Wake up and smell the coffee* instead of *pay attention.* Some other word-wasters are:

- *give a free hand* instead of *give permission*
- *keep your shirt on* instead of *calm down*
- *settle a score* instead of *retaliate*
- *much ado about nothing* instead of *fuss*
- *face like a wet weekend* instead of *sad*
- *bone of contention* instead of *disagreement*
- *more fun that a barrel of monkeys* instead of *funny*
- *running to the tall grass* instead of *escaping*
- *below the radar* instead of *not visible*

SAID BOOKISMS

These show up in dialog tags as replacements for *said* and *asked.* Here's an example: *"This invention will never amount to anything," Laura opined.*

In this sentence, *Laura opined* is the dialog tag, and *opined* is the bookism.

Note how the dialog itself shows us it's Laura's opinion. Then the author tells us it was her opinion by adding the tag *Laura opined.* This is duplication in the same sentence. The way to avoid this is to use *said.* Readers can determine the speaker's intent by reading the dialog. There's no need to remind them by adding a tag to repeat the same idea.

Q49: Identify the dialog tag in this sentence: *"I hate you," Joey growled.*

Q50: Which word in this sentence is the said bookism? *"Go home,"* *Barbara articulated.* _____

The reason for avoiding said bookisms is to keep readers from stumbling over unusual bookisms, causing them to pause. When readers pause even for a moment, they are thrown out of the story. If this happens too many times, the reader may put the story down and never complete it.

Here's another example: *"If you don't save for a rainy day, you'll be sorry," she advised.* In this case the dialog shows her intent to advise. The tag then tells us the same thing.

Look at this example: *"Shut your mouth!" Jim cut her off.* Not only do we have the bookism *cut her off,* but we also have a form of repetition. The dialog gives us the idea that Jim is cutting somebody's dialog off. Then the narrative tells us the same thing.

The same thing happens in this sentence: *"Stop it!" Anna begged.*

This example illustrates a bookism that shows up quite often, *"Being around you is like being around a barrel of monkeys," she laughed.*

Notice that this sentence not only includes a bookism, but also an idiomatic expression. The bookism points out a logic flaw that few ever notice: suggesting that anybody can laugh an 11-word sentence. They might say it, then laugh. Or they might laugh first, then say the words. But nobody can do both simultaneously.

Said bookisms also include adverbs, such as *profoundly, sweetly*, and many others. Sometimes the result looks quite odd, as shown in these examples:

- *"I won't go out with you," she hissed chillily.*
- *"I'm awake," Cindie said, opening her eyes groggily.*
- *"No!" Martha expressed firmly.*
- *"It's almost stopped raining," Adam offered helpfully.*
- *"Maybe they're the crazy ones," my roommate suggested enthusiastically.*

Here's a partial list of some bookisms that make editors frown:

breathed	*inquired*	*insisted*
crowed	*lied*	*sputtered*
enunciated	*laughed*	*absently*
enquired	*growled*	*angrily*
thundered	*sneered*	*evasively*
begged	*offered*	*icily*
shrieked	*asserted*	*seethed sarcastically*
spat back	*stated*	*demanded*
observed	*howled*	*snorted*

More examples, as they are used in dialog:

- *"I'm not your friend!" The man shrilled.*

- *Eddie, tell me a bit about yourself," Greta Bishop directed.*

- *You sure look like you need some," I said, affecting a shoddier grammar.*

- *"Never had this problem with the long boats," he growled.*

- *"I know what it is," he said patiently.*

- *"Don't," Cassie simply said.*

- *We artists are always misunderstood," declared Kevin.*

- *"Really!" he exclaimed in passionate excitement.*

Q51: Identify the said bookism in this sentence: *"Jump off the bridge,"* *she dared.* _____

Q52: Identify the said bookism in this sentence: *"This vitamin drink is making me feel like King Kong," he said zestfully.*

_____

Q53: Based on what you've seen in this lesson, which of the following has the potential for wasting the most words in a single sentence? Circle the answer.
> a. Foreign words
> b. Idiomatic expressions
> c. Slang
> d. Said bookisms

Q54: True or False: Forming a contraction saves 2 words. _____

Q55: Which is a characteristic of slang?
> a.It's perfect for FF.
> b.It's always current.
> c.It makes the read more enjoyable.
> d.It can date your story.

Q56: The word chillily is an example of:
> a.Said bookisms
> b.Needless repetition
> c.Slang
> d.Idiomatic expression

Q57: Name one of the negative effects to your story when you include regional dialog.

66

TELLING HOW CHARACTERS SPEAK

Another kind of word-waster is when we tell readers how a character spoke a line of dialog. Here's an example: *"What happened?" I blurted the question, not really wanting to know, but needing to know.*

In this example the word *blurted* tells how the character speaks. Whether or not the character blurted has no bearing on the plot, so it's a target for deletion. Same with all the words following *blurted*.

A way around this particular situation is to add another line of dialog. For example: *"What happened? I need to know."* This gives the same idea in less words.

As you read more examples, ask yourself if you care how the person spoke their dialog? Does it matter to the outcome of the story? If the answer is no, then you've read filler that wastes words in a FF tale. Let's look at more...

- *He spoke carefully.*
- *She answered calmly enough.*
- *He asked, transfixed.*
- *I worked up a serious but kind voice and said...*
- *The voice was low and sibilant in their heads.*
- *He said it with the voice of a silver-tongued devil with a trace of a British accent.*
- *I asked, trying to keep it professional.*
- *She said it with an unpleasant smile.*
- *The deputy sputtered something.*
- *I ask, raising my voice over the store's alarm.*
- *Trying not to blurt out, I gave him my name.*
- *She said it with a lively snap of her fingers.*
- *He spoke with stern conviction.*
- *He spit the last words out like acid or bitter wine.*
- *She leaned forward in her chair and whispered conspiratorially...*
- *Raising her voice to confront his emotional turmoil she said...*
- *Her voice was monotone as if she wasn't aware of the musical qualities inherent in human vocal cords.*
- *Rebecca spoke in her usual melodic tone.*

- *His voice was as measured and harsh as ever, but somehow Sergio thought he almost detected disappointment.*
- *Her voice was a high-pitched squall.*
- *The girl asked with hope in her voice.*

Q58: Eliminate superfluous details and rewrite: *"Look," Pete said, using a harsh whisper that reeked of insincerity, "I promise you this won't hurt at all."*

>

Q59: Do the same with these two sentences:
"Oh," Freddie said.
Kate went back to wiping the counter with her favorite dishrag. It was pink with splotches of bleach all over it.

>

Here's a summary of what we covered in this lesson:

Word-wasters that affect dialog that include:

- Trivial details.
- Words that can be converted to contractions.
- Repetition.
- Unnecessary interruptions.
- Slang.
- Foreign words.
- Regional dialects.
- Idiomatic expressions.
- Said bookisms.
- Describing how characters speak.

This concludes Lesson-5.

LESSON-6

WORD-WASTERS IN NARRATIVE – PART 1

This lesson discusses the following:

- Definition of trivial details

- Varieties of trivial details

- Trivial details as filler

DEFINTION OF TRIVIAL DETAILS

A trivial detail is any detail in the story that's not vital to the plot. Here's an example: *After a night's sleep, he headed for the nearest furniture store, which was a town away.* The trivial details are:

- *Nearest.* Whether the store was close or far is of no consequence.

- *Which was a town away.* Another meaningless fact.

The total number of wasted words in this sentence is 6.

In flash, it's enough to tell us he woke up and went to a furniture store. The location of the story and distance are trivial details. Deleting them results in this sentence: *After a night's sleep, he headed for a furniture store.* Cutting 6 words didn't affect the idea.

Here's another: *Around the building were beautiful red and white rose bushes, petunias, daffodils, poppies, and peonies.*

Q60: How would you rewrite this sentence to eliminate trivial details?

Q61: How many words are in your new sentence?

Q62: Rewrite to eliminate trivial details. *Betty's husband of fifty-seven years, two months, and thirteen days claimed a woman her age didn't need a racing car.*

```


```

Q63: How many words did you delete? _____

In this example, a man has just received an envelope from a courier. This sentence came next: *Holding the envelope loose in his left hand, he stood in the doorway of Room 411 in the Country Inns & Suites and watched the delivery girl saunter down the green-carpeted hallway, black-clad, teardrop-shaped hips swaying.*

Examine this 36-word sentence for trivial details and ask yourself the following questions:

- Does it matter which hand he uses to hold the envelope?

- Does it matter how he held it loosely?

- Does it matter that we were told he used his hand to hold something, considering holding implies the use of hands?

- Does it matter how the girl walked?

- Does the color of the carpet matter?

- Does the color of her clothing matter?

- Does it matter how her hips were shaped?

- Does it matter if her hips swayed when she walked?

We hope your answer is "No," to every question.

We wondered why the author wrote all these trivial details that lead to nowhere, instead of telling us the character opened the envelope, what he saw inside, and how he reacted. All this long sentence accomplished was to slow the read with trivial details that were superfluous to the plot.

Q64: How would you rewrite this sentence to eliminate all trivial details? *Holding the envelope loose in his left hand, he stood in the doorway of Room 411 in the Country Inns & Suites and watched the delivery girl saunter down the green-carpeted hallway, black-clad, teardrop-shaped hips swaying.* Hint: Use as many sentences as necessary to retain the ideas.

Another example: *They lay relaxing on the big four-poster bed. Both held a glass of champagne; the decanter on the bedside table showed itself only half full.* Ask yourself these questions.

- Does it matter to the story what kind of bed it was? If not, delete *the big four-poster.*

- Does it matter that they were relaxing?

- Does it matter to the plot where the decanter was located?

- Does it matter to the plot how much champagne remains in the decanter?

If none of these matter, the sentence could be rewritten like this: *They lay in bed, holding glasses of champagne.* The sentence is reduced by 17 words.

This example shows how closely you'll have to examine your work to ensure you didn't include any trivia. Remember: any FF tale overloaded with trivial details becomes a slow, boring read. Further, the more details, the less plot.

VARITIES OF TRIVIAL DETAILS

The kinds of trivial details that show up in FF are countless. However, many we've observed repeatedly in thousands of stories give trivial details about:

- Body movements

- Clothing

- What characters look like

- Getting around

- The environment

Let's look at some examples...

BODY MOVEMENTS

These show up almost anywhere in FF. They are always fillers, and slow down the read.

Example: *Running her finger gently down my cheek she leans up and gives me one more quick kiss, then pulls away and moves to the stove. She pokes at the eggs with a spatula.*

It's enough to tell us she kissed the character, the story should proceed to the next significant event. Reports of running fingers down cheeks, leaning, moving, pulling away, and poking make the read a yawner. Fillers like this abound in novels and short stories. Unfortunately, they show up all too frequently in flash fiction and are contrary to minimalist objectives.

Example: *She's crouched on the floor by the window, her arms wrapped tightly around her knees. Tilting her tear stained face up to me, she unwraps one of her arms and reaches out with her fingertips, tentatively.*

- Is it important to know exactly where she's situated?
- Is the presence of the window vital to the plot?
- Does it matter where her arms are?
- Does it matter if she tilts her face upward?
- Does it matter that she reaches out with one arm?

This might work if the author said: *She's crouching with arms wrapped around knees.*

Example: *Johnny moved over to his side stiffly, like I had slapped him in the face. He stared at me with icy eyes, curling his lips into a smile.* When dropping all the nonessential details, we get: *Johnny moved over to his side.*

Q65: How would you rewrite these sentences the minimalist way? *Looking down at her, I see her eyes cloud over. Almost go vacant. Then they seem to light up, and she smiles at me.*

DESCRIPTIONS OF CLOTHING

What characters wear is usually of no consequence in FF. Here's an example: *Alfred had on a navy waterproofed jacket with a drawstring hood tied up under his chin.*

If we drop the nonessential details and rewrite the sentence, we get: *Alfred wore a jacket.* Notice we also reduced word count by changing *had on* to *wore*. Means the same thing, but in less words.

Another example: *The bartender looked dignified in his tuxedo shirt and black bow tie.* These words were wasted, because the bartender wasn't even a minor character. The entire sentence should have been omitted.

Here's another example: *She wore a khaki skirt with a navy blouse that was belted in the middle, and brown espadrille wedges.*

We've noticed that when women authors include details about clothing, they often forget their audience includes men. We figure few men know what espadrille wedges are. We were thrown out of the story when we saw this description.

WHAT CHARACTES LOOK LIKE

Don't waste words telling us exactly what characters look like, even when they're monsters.

Example: Notice how far this 53-word description goes. *There he sat an ugly, gnome-like man. A lumpy face was crowded with thickened features. His lips protruded, and spittle was forming at the corners of his down turned mouth. A bulbous, red nose hung like a beak dominating its landscape. Two beady eyes peered out from underneath overgrown eyebrows.*

It's enough to tell FF readers a character is ugly. Everybody understands ugliness.

Example: *A fountain of sparks flared from the bonfire illuminating her face in gold.*

This is inflated prose to describe what a character looked like. It's from the realm of poetry, but we aren't writing poetry in FF.

Example: *I could see he was angry. Colour had fled from his eyes. They were empty as an Atlantic storm.*

Several problems with this one. First, we assume in a first person tale, the protagonist sees everything, so there's no need to remind us. It would've been enough to say: *He was angry.* However, a simile is also inserted comparing empty eyes to a storm on the Atlantic Ocean. This simile threw us out of the story, because we never saw anybody's eyes that were empty, much less looked like an ocean storm. We suspect a storm over the Atlantic is quite full of clouds, waves, and rain.

THE ENVIRONMENT

Many stories include trivial details about the environment.

Here's an example: *Floor to ceiling windows looked out over the eastward skyline and there were little white lights wrapped around the various potted bushes and palms that were lined up along the exposed brick walls. There was a white curtain strung in front of an alcove at one end and at the other end was a long table covered in a black cloth with all kinds of fruits and cheeses and crackers spread out all over it.*

This paragraph contains 75 words. Other paragraphs burned up over 150 more words on trivialities. The story was 885 words long. Thus, about 25% of the word count was wasted, resulting in a story with no plot.

GETTING AROUND

Trivial details describing how character move their bodies or body parts abound not only in dialog action tags, but also in narrative. They are usually associated with mundane activities and tend to be needless fillers.

Example: *James stood and carefully made his way to the kitchen sink where he rinsed out his cup and placed it in the dishwasher.*

We have to ask the following questions about this sentence and how pertinent they would be to any FF story:

- Is it necessary to tell readers James stood up? If he was sitting, then decided to head for the kitchen sink, he obviously had to stand up first. We can assume that without the author wasting words telling us.

- Is it necessary to say he made his way carefully? All he's doing is going to the kitchen, not through a dangerous mine field.

- Is it necessary to have him put the cup in the dishwasher? If he just puts it on a counter, then words wouldn't be wasted telling us he had to rinse the cup before putting it in the dishwasher.

The way to avoid all this is to tell readers James went to the kitchen and put his cup on the counter.

Example: *I swung around and went back into the hotel.*

Does it matter what he had to do with his body first, before he went back to the hotel? If he hadn't performed that needless ritual does that mean he couldn't reenter the hotel?

Q66: Rewrite this sentence to eliminate the wasted words: *I swung around and went back into the hotel.*

```
```

Q67: This one needs a bit of rewrite to drop wasted words: *Joe spread out his hands and reached toward me.*

```
```

Example: *I sighed and followed, shrugging my shoulders at the crowd of friends who watched as I followed Joe outside to his car.*

Notice the needless reports of sighing, shrugging, and watching. The idea here is that the character followed Joe outside to his car. The rest is word-wasting filler that burns up 15 words needlessly.

Q68: Fix this sentence: *Anna glared at Bob, and then at the top of her father's head, then decided to leave.*

```
```

Q69: Notice how many things have to happen before the character can get to the window. Rewrite without the trivial details. *Arching her back, she stood and walked to the window.*

```
```

Q70: Delete the trivial details in this sentence and rewrite: *Nora twisted her head and peeked out to see if Sam was coming.*

```



```

Q71: Fix this sentence: *From the corner of his eye, he watched the boat sail by.*

```



```

Example: *a dainty slip of a woman trips across to where I am standing, a smile glued into place. My hands droop at my side, like dead fish, and my legs seem to encompass a half of the room.*

Q72: What would you omit and how would you rewrite the sentences above?

```



```

Here's a summary of what we discussed in this lesson:

- Definition of trivial details

- Varieties of trivial details

- Editing sentences containing trivial details

This concludes Lesson-6.

LESSON-7

WORD-WASTERS IN NARRATIVE – PART 2

This lesson discusses the following word-wasters that appear in narratives:

- Inflated prose
- Similes

INFLATED PROSE

Inflated prose occurs in FF is when we use too many words to tell a simple fact.

Here's an example: *Her canteen had given up its last bit of water at 9AM that morning, and since then she had not seen as much as a hint of water.*

Buried in this 28-word story are the following facts:

- Her canteen was empty since 9 AM.

- She didn't see any water since then.

Instead of saying *her canteen was empty at 9 AM*, the author used excessive words to say *her canteen had given up its last bit of water at 9 AM that morning.* That's 15 words to tell what could've been said in 7.

One of the things to delete is *that morning* which is superfluous. 9 AM lets us know it happened in the morning.

Look at this one: *After returning to his neighborhood by city transit train, he stopped in at his regular neighborhood tavern and ordered a bar whiskey and a draft beer, the usual, and put it on his tab.* Too many details to tell us *he got home by train, went to the neighborhood bar, ordered a drink, and had it added to his tab.* The original has 34 words. We reduced it to 20.

Here's another example: *The sun is beginning to peek over the pines across the street.* The author used too many words to tell us the sun rose.

Another example: *I felt pride, as I committed it to the post office.* The words *committed it* substituted for the word *took.*

Examine this sentence:

> BEFORE: *Hildie plopped her ample bottom down on the curb, yanked her jogging shoe off, and worked the sweat-soaked sock away from her heel.*

> AFTER: *Hildie sat on the curb and removed one of her shoes and socks.*

The first sentence of 23 words was by a writer who isn't a story teller. The second, consisting of 13 words, was written by someone who emphasizes storytelling.

Identify inflated prose in the following sentences, delete, then rewrite.

Q73: *Joe was starting to see things.* Hint: use a word that means *to see things* in the context that Joe was having abnormal psychological reactions.

```

```

Q74: *Helen made her way to the park.*

```

```

Q75: *When sunrise whispered to the dead ground to wake, Nora crawled out of her boulder-protected cave.*

```

```

Q76: *The clown received a laughing reaction from the crowd.*

Q77: *Frank went so far as to order a drink.*

Q78: *Sam thought he was going to lose his cereal right there on the spot.*

Q79: *This signal flare of an idea lit her mind.*

Q80: *Fred saw a black weight in his eyes, a flash of something like hate.*

Q81: *The car rolled toward them at a sedate pace.*

Q82: *Her stony expression melted into a blush.*

Q83: *Denny jerked his head in the direction she was pointing and found a slightly short, chubby boy.*

Q84: *Harold turned a deaf ear to Nancy's protest.*

Q85: *She was small in height.*

Q86: *He started talking to himself, out of a sheer need for company.*

Q87: *Ambling along as I'm wont to do, stick jutting from my hand, a peculiar odor snatches up my senses.*

Q88: *He took yet another glance towards the main entrance.*

Let's move on to a discussion of how similes waste words in FF…

SIMILES

Don't waste time and word count devising similes and including them in your FF. Here's why:

- Many don't achieve the effect the author intended.

- They draw attention to themselves, especially when they don't work.

- When they're poorly conceived, they can throw readers out of the story.

- They're word-wasters.

- It isn't necessary to amplify something that was said by adding a simile. For example, it's enough to tell us a character is angry. Readers understand what that means. It isn't necessary to waste words saying she's as mad as a hornet whose nest was just wacked with a broomstick.

- Sometimes we get the impression authors aren't confident in their ability to say something that's mundane, clearly enough. Seems they add a simile to ensure we know for sure what they mean. As noted above, it isn't necessary to further clarify what it means for somebody to be angry. The simile attempts to tell the degree to which the character was angry by comparing it with a hornet's anger. In flash that's overkill. It's enough for flash readers to know a character was angry.

Here's a simile from a story: *Quickly, he was on his knees prying at the lock like a starving puppy.*

When we read this, we were thrown out of the story. We think it's easy for readers to visualize what a man looks when he's on his knees, trying to open a lock, without invoking the sorrowful image of a starving puppy.

Here's another simile that didn't work for us because it was too cryptic: *She was curved into herself, like a spiral of a dream.* A simile such as this might work very nicely in poetry, but not in the narrative of a flash tale. It threw us out of the story, as we stopped reading to figure out what the author meant. This frustrates one of the ideals of FF: a story that can be read as quickly as possible.

Here are more similes that threw us out of the stories in which they appeared.

- *The fire hydrant sputtered a few times like a mocking little red demon.*

- *She looked at me like we were on an airplane and she hoped I'd shut up*

- *Suddenly, the Armadillo 3000 listed hard to port as the cutting blades caught on the edge of an abyss like a drill bit emerging from the bottom of a piece of wood.*

- *His brain fired like tumblers in a lock.*

- *Holding my breath in anticipation of disaster, I opened it cautiously like a coroner dissecting a mangled murder victim.*

- *While the pain continued like tuning forks to pierce her head, Jamie felt herself slide off and divide into three.*

- *A trail of woman's clothes, from blouse to panties, was strewn across the floor like Hansel and Gretel's breadcrumbs, leading into the bedroom.*

- *His skin stung, burning like a pig on a spit, blistering and swelling painfully.*

- *Before he could move or make a sound, it crushed him like he was a Dixie cup.*

- *As soon as the helicopter breached the tree level, it leaned forward like an eager drunk.*

- *Its words absorbed into his frontal lobes like a willow tree sucking up rain after a storm.*

Now that you've read all these similes, perhaps you understand why minimalists omit them from FF.

Here's a summary of what we covered in this lesson:

- Definition of inflated prose

- Examples of inflated prose

- Exercises in detecting inflated prose

- Exercises in deleting inflated prose

- Exercises in rewriting inflated prose

- A review of similes

- Why similes waste words in flash fiction

This concludes Lesson-7.

LESSON-8

WORD-WASTERS IN NARRATIVE – PART 3

This lesson discusses the following word-wasters that appear in narratives.

- Long sentences

- Repetition

- Facts of Existence

LONG SENTENCES

Including long sentences in FF is contrary to minimalist objectives. Therefore, you should avoid them.

Let's examine some that we've seen in FF. Then we'll ask you to convert them to two or more sentences.

Here's an example of a 42-word sentence: *And so it was that in her fifteenth year, Mary Brown formed her secret pact with the rock star whose only connection with her had been in the form of an autographed picture she'd asked for years earlier in a fan letter.*

Let's examine the information in this sentence. To rewrite it, we must include the information the writer wishes to convey to the reader. Here are the essential elements of information we gleaned from this long sentence:

- Mary Brown formed a secret pact with an unnamed rock star.

- She made the pact on the strength of an autographed picture.

- She had never met the rock star.

- She had written him a fan letter years before she was fifteen, but we aren't told how old she was when she wrote the letter.

- She had received an autographed photo in return.

Q89: Write two or more sentences to include the facts listed in this sentence: *And so it was that in her fifteenth year, Mary Brown formed her secret pact with the rock star whose only connection with her had been in the form of an autographed picture she'd asked for years earlier in a fan letter.* Reduce word count by removing unnecessary details.

Here's a 23-word sentence that doesn't work on two levels. It's too long, and it's loaded with inflated prose. *With it being the middle of August, the humidity of summer's end draped over the city, smothering the citizens under its heavy blanket.* This sentence gives 3 facts:

- The story is set in the middle of August.

- Humidity was high.

- Citizens felt smothered by the humidity.

The rest of the information is superfluous. In fact it may be unnecessary to pinpoint exactly when in August this incident occurred. We can generalize by just saying *August.* Also, the sentence has erroneous information when it states the middle of August was equal to the end of summer. Summer doesn't end until the third week of September, which is beyond the middle of August. That's a nit, but some readers may react unfavorably to this inaccuracy.

Q90: The 23-word sentence is repeated: *With it being the middle of August, the humidity of summer's end draped over the city, smothering the citizens under its heavy blanket.* Rewrite it to include the 3 facts we listed on the previous page. Reduce word count by omitting unnecessary details and incorrect information about summer's end. Note that the opening phrase is awkward: *With it being the middle of August.* Consider deleting it.

This one's 31 words long: *It looked a bit awkward since he was extremely tall and handsome, and she was a petite little thing with long brown tresses that dripped water on her cotton summer sundress.* The sentence gives the following essential facts:

- A man was extremely tall and handsome.

- A woman was short.

- Their height made them look awkward together.

Q91: Now that you've seen the 3 essential facts listed above, identify the trivial details in the sentence: *It looked a bit awkward since he was extremely tall and handsome, and she was a petite little thing with long brown tresses that dripped water on her cotton summer sundress.*

Sometimes we can cut too much from a sentence and make it sound choppy. This may distract and irritate readers. You can always test how smoothly sentences sound by reading aloud the original and the revised versions. When in doubt, include the sentence that sounds better.

REPETITION

Repetition is another word waster. Here's an example: *She lit the candles —she always lit candles when working on these special jobs.*

We only need to know once that she lit candles. Thus, the sentence could've been written this way to use as few words as possible: *She always lit candles when working on special jobs.*

More examples:

- *Harry was one of the...one of the fortunate ones.*
- *For the last few hours, the man had noticed something even more palpable—an ominous, eerie feeling, a feeling that he was being followed.*
- *And so they did wait. They waited and waited and waited.*

Here's an example that can't be repaired: *Kites are kites.*

FACTS OF EXISTENCE

Ordinary facts of everyday existence should not be included in a flash tale. For example, everyone knows the sun rises in the east. They also know people get wet when they walk without umbrellas on rainy days. Nevertheless, word-wasters like this show up in FF. Here are more examples:

- *Manny ran from the parking lot, the laughter fading the further away he got.*
- *Then, as with all living things, Bill and all his dogs got older.*
- *It was a dark night.*
- *Death comes to us all.*
- *Children go through so many stages and the teenage years are the hardest, they say.*

Here's a summary of what we covered in this lesson:

- Long sentences are often cumbersome and awkward in FF.
- Long sentences should be rewritten after deleting wasted words.
- Rewrite, ensuring you retain the original meaning.
- When rewriting long sentences you'll probably end up with more than 1 sentence.
- Ensure deletions don't create a choppy read.
- Read the new sentence out loud to see if it's smooth enough.
- Repetition wastes words.
- Telling readers things they already know wastes words.

This concludes Lesson-8.

WORD-WASTERS IN NARRATIVE – PART 4
LESSON-9

This lesson discusses the following word-wasters that appear in FF narratives.

- Telling then correcting

- Telling what isn't

- Flashbacks

- Cookbook procedures

TELLING THEN CORRECTING

One of the word-wasters is to tell us something, then correct it in the same sentence. Here's an example: *The jerk was still walking, (okay, limping).*

The author could've saved words by telling us: *The jerk was still limping.*

More examples:

- *Pale and cloudy eyes stared blankly at me—more like beyond me.*

- *The treasure was near one of the houses, near a large house actually.*

- *It was one of the produce stock boys. Only he wasn't a boy; he was a man.*

- *At the end of the street, she hit traffic. Well. Not traffic. Just a gardener's truck, stopped at the corner where no one ever stopped.*

- *However, five minutes before the town, I saw her! Actually, her smile —just as I went into the curve in the road, I sensed something that felt as reflection of a light beam.*

This one involves 3 sentences in which the author corrects himself twice: *It was Flag Day, three years ago, when my life came crushing down on me. Actually, not really on me, but on my husband. And it wasn't life that crushed him either; it was a 2009 Chrysler SUV.*

Q92: Rewrite the above to eliminate trivial details. Do it in 1 sentence.

Q93: Fix this sentence: *America is probably the greatest country in the world, no scratch that it is the greatest country world.*

Look at this one: *He was sitting in what appeared to be a gully, a trough nearly choked by the tendrils and roots of the jungle. But closer examination revealed it wasn't a gully at all—it was an alley.*

Q94: Rewrite using a single sentence: *He was sitting in what appeared to be a gully, a trough nearly choked by the tendrils and roots of the jungle. But closer examination revealed it wasn't a gully at all—it was an alley.*

More examples:

- *He was the handsomest boy Sally had ever seen. More accurately, he was the handsomest man she had ever seen.*

- *There she was dancing on the deck by the apartment complex pool, in her nightgown, or maybe it was her slip.*

When writing FF, don't say one thing, and correct what was just said. Remember that you're in control of everything you write.

TELLING WHAT ISN'T OR SOMEBODY DIDN'T DO

One of the more unusual waste of words in FF is when authors tell us things that characters didn't do, didn't think, or almost didn't do.

Here's an example of telling readers something that a character didn't do: *The zombie didn't stop walking.* This implies the zombie had been walking all along, so we wondered why the author chose this point in the story to remind us it was still walking.

More examples:

- *She wasn't a princess, nor was she beautiful.*
- *The stone face before him was no natural shelf or cliff, but the vine smothered facade of a building constructed eons ago.*
- *Without looking up she said...*
- *This story didn't happen in June, or July, or August. It happened in September.*
- *It was not fear that gripped Stephanie but sorrow.*
- *He was not tempted to examine the massive oaken table.*
- *The sun didn't rise and it didn't sink.*
- *Joe didn't laugh.*
- *Marcus groaned, not having to turn around.*
- *No wagons to unpack, no canvas to unroll, no reason to work.*
- *It didn't look immediately like this town, that was for sure.*
- *Shirley didn't get sick when The Magistrate entered with a game warden and his deputy.*
- *When Peter hit middle age, he was not so bothered by the chatter of insects.*
- *If that bothered her, there was no sign.*
- *She also does not see the $1.52 check for her Sprite in a red plastic Coca-Cola cup, nor does she notice that everyone else has left; only that he never arrived.*
- *It didn't slam against her, winding with sudden force.*
- *She stopped at the bedroom door, but didn't turn around.*
- *It's not that his Friday night game makes life unbearable.*

In this example, somebody *almost* did something, which means they didn't do it: *As I shut the car door, I noticed the flashing had stopped and I nearly returned to the car but then the restaurant door opened, smoothly and quietly.*

We question the need to waste words in FF to tell readers somebody nearly did something in a scene. The word nearly still means they didn't perform the act. Most of these sentences can't be rewritten.

Look at this one: *He didn't speak of his wife, he spoke of his daughter.* Words were wasted telling us who he didn't talk about. It's enough to tell us: *He spoke of his daughter.* We'll understand that nobody else was mentioned.

Rewrite the following sentences:

Q95: *He heard the sound of a single aircraft but didn't look up.*

>

Q96: *She stopped at the bedroom door, but didn't turn around.*

>

FLASHBACKS

This FF word-waster moves the story backward instead of forward. That's contrary to the ideal FF tale, which is supposed to move forward at all times.

Here's an example in which the author opens with a grabber, then suddenly gives us a flashback, also known as backstory:

> *Joe decided to rob the town's only bank. On the way, he remembered the first time he robbed a bank back in 1950. That's when a buck was a buck, and $2,000 bought a full size, eight-cylinder Chevy.*
> *Back then, he used to go with Elsie, whose dad also robbed banks. In fact, Joe and her dad took the First National Bank for a cool hundred thousand.*
> *There were other robberies through the years. But he got caught in 1960.*

The story begins with the idea that Joe was on his way to rob a bank. We expected to read more about this criminal adventure, but instead Joe started thinking about his bank robbing history that began in 1950. Then several hundred words were expended on a history lesson. Meanwhile, the story moved backward, instead of forward. By the time Joe got to rob the bank, not enough words were left to make the scene compelling.

If authors insist on letting us know a bit about a character's past, we suggest they do it in a couple sentences. Here's an example: *Joe decided to rob the town's only bank. This would be the twentieth bank he robbed, since he started his criminal career in 1950.* This gives the idea that Joe is a career criminal. The next sentence should continue with Joe being on his way to rob a bank.

Another way to handle this is to begin the story with his first bank robbery in 1950, and take it forward from there.

If a story is about, say, a distraught person about to jump off a bridge, it's okay if a character asks why. The protagonist can give a short answer, then the story should move forward to its conclusion.

On the other hand, if a writer decides to take readers back to, say, three months ago, and detail how the protagonist was abandoned by the woman he loved, the story has gone backward. It's enough for the jumper to say he lost his girlfriend. Then the story should move forward.

Q97: From the minimalist point of view, why should we omit flashbacks from FF tales?

COOKBOOK PROCEDURES

This kind of word-waster occurs when authors describe every step a character performs to accomplish a task. This kind of detail always stalls a FF tale.

Here's the first example: *Jolene removed the tablecloth, and spread newspapers across the kitchen table. After carrying the pumpkin inside, she traced a scary face on its broadest side with a magic marker. Then, Jolene grabbed the carving knife, and guided it around the top.*

The minimalist approach reduces the 41 words and 3 sentences to 13 words in a single sentence: *Jolene put a pumpkin on the kitchen table and carved a scary face.* We cut so much, because this is loaded with trivial details:

- She removed the table cloth.

- She spread newspapers across the kitchen table.

- She carried the pumpkin inside to carve it.

- She used the broadest side of the pumpkin to trace a face.

- She grabbed a knife to do this, as it's understood you must use a knife to carve a pumpkin.

- She guided the knife around the top.

Q98: Write 1 sentence to remove the procedures. Keep the main ideas.

```



```

Another example. This one expends 42 words giving us a procedure in great detail: *Stanley pulled on his worn slacks, and the equally worn flannel shirt. He slipped his feet into a pair of high topped shoes. He slept in his socks to keep his feet warm. Then he trudged down the hall to the bathroom.*

This sentence contains 44 words. *She takes a packet of chocolate chip cookies from the cupboard, eats one, then another, and then another, faster and faster, stuffing one after another into her mouth, chewing, swallowing, like something starved for a long, long time, until every last one is eaten.*

The verb *gobble* describes what the character did. Here's one way to reduce this sentence: *She grabs a box of cookies and gobbles them.* Readers know what gobbling is, so there's no need to burn up word count giving excruciating details.

Look at this one: *Hank shoved the door shut, walked over to the rumpled bed and sat. He turned the envelope over, studied the address and the blurred, red October 31 postmark. He slid a blunt, thick finger under the flap, wincing when the paper caught a ragged cuticle. He pulled out two sheets and unfolded them, angling the second to read the lawyer's signature.*

Q99: Rewrite the sentences shown above the minimalist way.

Q100: This one's loaded with trivial details: *He went back to his room, slipped on the only sweater he had, a heavy wool sweater with holes at the elbows, picked up his shopping bag full of books, and tiptoed into the dark kitchen.* Reduce word count and rewrite.

Q101: How would you rewrite this 15-word sentence to eliminate the cookbook procedure: *Sally stopped, unloaded, and retrieved the purple, virgin journal from her tattered, navy blue backpack.*

Q102: Rewrite this one to reduce it to as few words as possible: *He stepped on a pedal and opened a stainless steel trashcan, then threw the empty cartridge from the hypodermic needle into it.*

Q103: Rework this one: *He started the car motor, shifted into drive, and we pulled out of the parking lot, into the street.*

Another example: *He'll rush home from work soon; throw his briefcase on the hall table and his tie on top of it. Bounding up the stairs, three at a time, he'll disappear into our bedroom, change out of his work clothes and be ready to go. Avoiding eye contact, he'll edge toward the door, muttering that we should ask Ted and Alice to do something tomorrow night. Maybe dinner, or a movie.*

As you can imagine, this story had no plot, and was the opposite of what we wish to achieve as minimalists.

Final example. This one burns up 50 words. *Jason finished his coffee, scrubbed, dried and put the mug back into the glass fronted cabinet, poured vinegar into the coffee maker, flushed it with hot water seven times, rubbed the chrome and glass streak-free, put the shining machine back into its nook and headed off to start his day.*

The author could have saved dozens of words and avoided reader boredom by telling us: *Jason finished his coffee and left his apartment.*

Here's a summary of what we covered in this lesson:

- How telling then correcting wastes words.

- How telling what isn't wastes words.

- Most sentences telling what isn't can't be rewritten.

- How flashbacks waste words.

- How to give a little bit of past information about a character.

- How cookbook procedures waste words.

This concludes Lesson-9.

LESSON-10

WORD-WASTERS IN NARRATIVE – PART 5

This lesson discusses the following word-wasters that appear in FF narratives.

- Sluggish character movements

- Superfluous pauses

- Watching, glancing, glaring

- Turning

- Impossible mannerisms

SLUGGISH CHARACTER MOVEMENTS

This occurs when authors use too many words to get characters through doors, in and out of buildings, or from one point to another in any setting.

In this example, the author tells how a character got to the front door after somebody knocked: *I walked down the hallway to the front door and there was Neville standing on the doorstep with a couple of bags.*

This can be reduced to: *I opened the front door and saw Neville holding some bags.* The new sentence omits the following trivial details:

- The protagonist walking down a hallway to reach the door.

- Neville was standing.

- Exactly where he was standing.

Look at this example: *Jean slid off her chair to the tiled kitchen floor and walked slowly towards the open back door. She stopped three tiles short of it and leaned forward, trying to see out around the doorpost.*

Q104: Delete trivial details from the procedure above, and write a single sentence.

Here's another example: *Getting out of his car, Frank walked up to the back door of the bar, unlocking the door and entering the building.* This example burns up 18 words to get him from the car into the building.

Q105: How would you rewrite the sentence shown above?

Q106: Fix this one: *I got up and went over to the table where Mary was sitting.* Hint: Use a possessive noun and try to do it in 5 words.

Q107: *Harry stepped out of the jewelry store.* Rewrite this one to cut 2 words to get Harry from point A to point B: *Harry stepped out of the jewelry store.*

This example shows how to stall a FF tale while describing how a character gets from point A to point B: *He walked to work, the same route 5 days a week, so familiar he could do it blindfolded. Past the coffee shop, past the post office, past the pet grooming salon he once thought read saloon, past the bench where sits Gus, expressionless, eyes heaven bound.*

The author used 46 words, which is far too many for any flash tale. When we cut out all the filler in this cookbook procedure, we ended up with this: *His route to work was so familiar, he could do it blindfolded.*

Here's one that uses dialog and narrative to create a complicated entrance.

> *"May I come in?"*
> *"What? Oh yes of course. I'm very sorry, where are my manners? Please come in. Come in.*
> *He stepped aside and granted her passage. She stepped in and he turned to follow her.*

This kind of writing slows down the read. The way to handle this is to say: *She invited him inside.* That cuts 33 words from the original.

Let's move on to superfluous pauses...

SUPERFLOUS PAUSES

These word-wasters occur when authors make their characters stop all activities within a scene. This shouldn't be done in FF, because stories are supposed to move forward as quickly as possible.

This list shows pauses we've seen in FF. As you read them, ask yourself if it was necessary to waste words pausing a character's activities.

- *We sit for a moment, staring at a small yellow bungalow. He hadn't moved.*

- *Eric stopped for a moment to think.*

- *Pat slowly stood up and walked over to my fireplace.*

- *Arthur gazed at May for a brief moment before he turned away from her.*

- *The handsome man paused near an elderly couple.*

- *He paused to grin at a blond co-ed entering the classroom.*

- *He paused when he saw Joe brush the back of his hand across his eyes.*

- *She paused, pondered her thoughts and carefully said...*

- *He slowed his pace to wipe his face and then got back into step.*

- *He paused in thought. After a moment he added...*

- *He waited till she sat down before taking a seat himself.*

- *I stood frozen, my eyes glued to the man.*

- *The man paused again and turned to the western sunshine.*

- *Kayla' eyes finally met Dylan's.*

- *She paused for a moment, thinking.*

- *Freddie got up from the kitchen table and stared at her mother's back for a little while.*

- *Gordy sat silent for a moment.*

Let's pull one from the list and see what we can do with it: *He paused to grin at a blond co-ed entering the classroom.*

The character could've grinned at the co-ed without pausing. Rewriting the sentence this way saves 2 words and omits the pause: *He grinned at a blond co-ed entering the classroom.*

Most pauses we've seen in FF tales can't be fixed. They should never have appeared in the first place. They only burned up word count that could've been put to better use in the story. Consequently, there are no practice exercises to rewrite these sentences.

WATCHING, GLANCING, GLARING

Another word-waster we often see is a report of characters glancing, glaring at, or watching other characters they've been interacting with in a scene. We find these reports unnecessary, because if characters populate a scene, we figure they must be watching each other to begin with. It's a given—something we don't have to be reminded of in the narrative. Here are some examples:

- *He watched her walk away for a minute, attention off the fire hydrant.*

- *Sandra watched him eat a cookie.*

- *She saw Sal's shoulder rise in the barest of shrugs.*

- *She watched him pack a can of tuna.*

- *Mandy gave the old man a cursory glance.*

- *Monica watched the old man's mouth open and close.*

- *He studied her for a moment and she returned his gaze, to show him she had nothing to hide.*

- *I watched as they small-talked.*

- *Grandpa's eyes looked over Joe and his cousin Lisa.*

- *Danny's uncle left the bedroom, shooting a warning glare back at him from the door.*

- *I glared back at him and then, in a stern voice said, "George. Sit down."*

- *He gave her an uncaring glare.*

- *Marcus shot a quick glance around.*

Some sentences can be salvaged when writing in third person. Let the omniscient narrator tell us, instead of a character. Let's use one of the sentences from the above list as an example:

BEFORE: *She watched him pack a can of tuna.*

AFTER: *He packed a can of tuna.*

This cuts 2 words without changing the meaning.

However, sentences like this example also include trivial filler, that should be removed: *Lester glared at Bill, clearly not appreciating the sarcasm. Bill glared back. He opened his eyes as wide as possible, and flares his nostrils, causing Lester to look away.*

Q108: See what you can glean from the sentence above and rewrite. Do it in 1 sentence.

Let's move on to the next word waster...

TURNING

We've read thousands of instances where characters have to turn first before doing something else in a story. All were superfluous.

For example, in a long dialog stream, suddenly we were told that a character turned to the other to say something. That gave the impression the characters hadn't been facing each other the entire time they'd been talking, which seemed illogical.

We think the only time a character should turn in a FF tale is when it's vital to the plot. For example, a character turns to avoid getting a bayonet slammed into his gut.

Here are some examples of turning that accomplish nothing except to burn up word count:

- *Then there was a high-pitched sound and the green creatures turned and left the house.*

- *He turned, sucking in his gut as he did.*

- *He turned toward the door, but Beatrice quickly got up and stopped him.*

- *The young man turned and stared at her.*

- *Then he turned to face her.*

- *The artist turned back to Kathy.*

- *She turned around and leaned back against the wall, hands in pockets, a study in tranquility.*

- *She sat down and glanced at Mike before turning to Aaron.*

- *I turned to him and took a step back shakily and looked down at his face.*

- *All three of their heads turn toward the hall as they hear a toilet flush.*

- *The aliens turned to the cameras, pulling away their false faces.*

- *He turned his back and laughed his snide little laugh.*

Let's take a look at one of them to see how we'd rewrite it:

BEFORE: *Then there was a high-pitched sound and the green creatures turned and left the house.*

AFTER: *Hearing a high pitched sound, the creatures left.*

Note that we didn't include *the house* because readers had been told earlier that the creatures were in a house. No need to be repetitious. It only burns up word count.

Q109: Fix this one: *Kate turned around and looked at Freddie, who was sitting at the kitchen table taking a quiz in her magazine.*

IMPOSSIBLE MANNERISMS

This one reports a character's mannerisms that seem impossible to perform. Here are some examples:

- *His eyes leered at her with a low level of expectation.*

- *He swallowed reactionary sympathy.*

- *He shrugged apologetically.*

- *She inhaled down to her belly button.*

- *She went, a look of half-finished wonder on her face*

- *She tentatively reached out toward him.*

- *Her lips turned up in a rueful smile.*

- *I smiled inwardly.*

- *He gave his audience a flustered smile.*

- *His client sunk into himself.*

- *The corners of the sheriff's mouth twitched, forming something just short of a smile.*

- *The blonde in the pink bodysheath nodded comfortably.*

- *He gave her a cocky, full-of-himself, smile.*

We always cite sentences like this in our critiques by saying, "If you can't look in a mirror and repeat these actions you attribute to your characters, don't include them in your stories."

There's no way to rewrite these word-wasting sentences, unless other actions are included. Here's an example of a sentence that can be saved: *I slammed the window shut and blinked back my own laughter.*

This can be rewritten like this: *I slammed the window shut.*

This kind of word-waster occurs when authors develop their stories as artistic writers, not storytellers. Descriptions like this would never be spoken when telling a story to a friend over coffee.

Here's a summary of what we covered in this lesson:

- Sluggish character movements

- Superfluous pauses

- Watching and glancing

- Turning

- Impossible mannerisms

This concludes Lesson-10, which is the last lesson in this book.

Word Reduction Exercises begin on the next page.

WORD REDUCTION EXERCISES

Figure out what the sentence means, and rewrite as necessary to save as many words a possible. Answers for this exercise are provided on page 124.

Q01: *He kept old tools in his workshop out back.*

Q02: *A smile creased his face.*

Q03: He could not, for the life of him, figure out what every client wanted.

Q04: *A scared whimper found its way out of his mouth.*

Q05: *The woman's face flashed a startled expression.*

Q06: *I dropped the ice bucket and ran back to my room.*

Q07: *I followed Bobby to his mansion with a pool and basketball court.*

Q08: *With a howl of pain, he collapsed to the pavement.*

Q09: *I opened my mouth, but let the words disappear.*

Q10: *The baker cowered back like a stuck dog.*

Q11: *I heard the police sirens as they pulled into the hotel parking lot.*

Q12: *The stench of his rotting flesh assaulted my nostrils.*

Q13: *There was nothing there.*

Q14: *When he got out of his car I shot him in the head, leaving him in a pool of blood.*

Q15: *The sword tore into the vampire's cold flesh slicing his head from the body.*

Q16: *The red numbers on the clock glowed 2:30.*

Q17: *The rain pelted the house, falling in sheets from the metal roof like a curtain drawn across a window.*

Q18: *He decided then to turn and confront them.*

Q19: *He walked toward the door, but Ellie quickly got up and stopped him.*

Q20: *She fixed the problem from the top to the bottom.*

Q21: *It was then that he found a shriveled, rotting lantern made from Landon's head.*

Q22: *Erika's face was as long as the day is long.*

Q23: *I arrived and put his body into the incinerator in the basement.*

Q24: *Raymond's eyes darted about the throngs of people whose heads were thrown back and howling with delight.*

Q25: *The pedestrians actually halted their comings and goings.*

Q26: *The applause from the audience gained in volume.*

Q27: *Jack affected a nod.*

Q28: *The pallor of her face spoke in green and grays of pain, exhaustion and sickness.*

Q29: *She didn't respond in voice but I felt her push with greater determination into the pulpy floor.*

Q30: *He relinquished his hold and looked into his wife's eyes.*

Q31: *The audience-members took to their feet for a standing ovation to honor the winner.*

Q32: *Phil had a taste for sweets and a penchant toward cruelty.*

Q33: *I thought I would feel bad murdering someone but I guess the silence made me feel as calm as I can be.*

Q34: *Her body began to succumb to the luxury of sleep.*

Q35: *I slid my engagement ring along my finger, slipped it off gently, and handed it to Johnny.*

Q36: *After drying her shoes, she slipped her feet into them and faced the mirror on the back of the bathroom door.*

Q37: *He never mentioned his wife, though he did speak of his daughters.*

Q38: *The old man stood a few feet from me on the sidewalk, sputtering and waving.*

Q39: *She was nothing but a ball of eccentricity.*

Q40: *After an episode of vomiting, he managed to push himself back to his feet.*

Q41: *Disgust was the first feeling he had once the shock wore off.*

Q42: *I could hear her cursing under her breath.*

Q43: *After exhaling a long blood-curdling scream of his own, he drove off.*

Q44: *Charlie consulted his book of science.*

Q45: *A young-looking attorney suddenly scurried out the door, his pale face etched in absolute terror.*

Q46: *A sudden burst of fatigue slowly passed over her form.*

Q47: *He kept licking his cracked bloody lips, not quite sure what was going on yet.*

Q48: *Rosie would hoot and start to laugh out loud.*

Q49: *To catch a smile on her face was becoming a rarity.*

Q50: *I noticed that George was sitting quietly now.*

ANSWER PAGES FOR LESSONS 1 THROUGH 10

Q01: 1,000 words

Q02: 1,000 to 10,000 and 40,000 on up.

Q03: Similes

Q04: They are never vital to the plot. They burn up word count unnecessarily.

Q05: They are never vital to the plot.

Q06: Any 6 of the following:

- It should tell a complete story that can be read in 5 minutes or less.

- It should have an opener that pulls readers into the story.

- It should be plot-driven.

- It should emphasize telling over showing.

- It should be a fast read.

- It should always move forward at a brisk pace.

- It should be free of inflated prose.

- It should be free of trivial details.

- It should be free of distractions that can throw readers out of the story.

- It should contain dialog.

- It should contain a maximum of 4 characters

- It should contain a maximum of 4 scenes

- It should end in a way that makes it complete.

Q07: Content

Q08: Any of these, plus many more not listed:

- Crime

- Mystery

- Romance

- Speculative

- Thriller

- War

- Western

Q09: To tell as much story as possible, in as few words as possible, without sacrificing a smooth read.

Q10: She took a blade to see how sharp it was. No need to mention she had to reach out to do this.

Q11: The girl grew very curious, but her grandmother wouldn't let her open the box or touch it.

Q12: He said goodbye to Deborah and left. Saves 5 words.

Q13: She sorted the mail. Saves 2 words.

Q14: Tightly written sentences make the story move forward faster. The ideal genre FF tale can be read in 5 minutes or less.

Q15: Telling

Q16: Telling generally uses fewer words in narrative than dialog. Less words means the tale moves forward faster. An objective of the minimalist was is to tell as much story as possible in as few words as possible. However, we want to do this in a way that ensures a smooth read.

Q17: Dialog

Q18. Plot-driven. Because of word count limitations, FF tales are plot-driven.

Q19: Events. In a plot-driven story, events take precedence.

Q20: They waste words, plus readers don't care about characters' last names, unless the character is famous, such as Abraham Lincoln.

Q21: It could throw readers out of the story.

Q22: You answer should have included any 4 of these dialog word wasters:

- Action tags
- Words that can be converted to contractions
- Repetition
- Unnecessary Interruptions
- Slang
- Foreign words
- Regional dialects
- Idiomatic expressions
- Said bookisms
- Descriptions of how characters speak

Q23: Your answer should have included any 6 of these narrative words wasters:

- Trivial details
- Inflated prose
- Similes
- Long sentences
- Repetition

- Facts of existence

- Telling then correcting

- Telling what isn't

- Flashbacks

- Cookbook procedures

- Sluggish movements

- Superfluous pauses

- Turning

- Watching and glancing

- Impossible mannerisms

Q24: Four scenes are ideal.

Q25: Four characters maximum.

Q26: Pompous prose can throw them out of the story. We never want that to happen.

Q27: In a red beret with a black woolen scarf. Doesn't matter what she's wearing.

Q28: 9 words.

Q29: A number of ways to do this. Our version: The family saw many tubes and plastic bags around the hospital patient.

Q30: We cut *Smith's, smooth, mahogany, like an ocean.* Last names don't matter in flash, unless the character is famous. *Smooth* and *mahogany* are trivia. *Like an ocean* is a simile that doesn't work for this sentence. We don't get the connection between a dry desk and a wet ocean. Also, desks are a few feet wide. Oceans are thousands of miles. We discuss problems with similes in Lesson-7.

Q31: Melvin was excited. He sat behind a desk.

Q32: Melvin was excited as he sat behind the desk.

Q33: Well-crafted dialog uses less words than narrative. We showed you some examples where this was true. Also, dialog can be more dramatic than narrative, as we showed in the mermaid scene.

Q34: A number of ways to do this. Our version:

"Can I kiss you?" Jason asked.

"No!"

Q35: A number ways to do this. Our version:

"I see a vampire!" somebody said.

"Run!" yelled Harold.

Q36: Any 5 of the following:

- Action tags
- Words that can be converted to contractions
- Repetition
- Unnecessary interruptions
- Slang
- Foreign words
- Regional dialects
- Idiomatic expressions
- Said bookisms
- Describing how characters speak

Q37: Any three of the following:

- They burn up lots of word count.
- They slow down the read.
- They can stall the read.
- They are distracting, because they often intrude and draw attention to themselves.
- They always contain trivial details that can get boring very quickly.
- They don't add anything of value to the plot.

Q38: Harry said, "I've had better." The rest is superfluous. No need to have him pause or scratching his cheek.

Q39: Our sentence saves 15 words.

Q40: They slow down the read. They make the story boring.

Q41: "She's a snob," Jones said.

Q42: We deleted 13 words: *a paunchy old man with thick glasses wearing a shrunken, grimy t-shirt, skulking.*

Q43: "I'll see you when I get there, but you'll have to make sure you're on time."

Q44: 3 contractions. I'll, you'll, you're.

Q45: "He loved to talk," Mary said.

Q46: This could be written many ways. Here's our two sentences of dialog:

"Really?"

"Yeah."

Q47: "I need to get home on the next plane," Lisa said.

Q48: "Why would somebody do that?"

Q49: Joey growled.

Q50: Articulated

Q51: *Dared* is the bookism. The author used it as a substitute for *said.*

Q52: *Zestfully* is the bookism. In this case it's an adverbial. Removing it saves 1 word.

Q53: Item b. Idiomatic expressions.

Q54: False. Forming a contraction saves 1 word.

Q55: Item d. It can date your story, because it changes constantly.

Q56: Item a. Said bookism.

Q57: Hard to read. Will throw readers out of the story.

Q58: "Look," said Pete, "I promise you this won't hurt."

Q59: "Oh," Freddie said. The rest is superfluous.

Q60: Beautiful flowers surrounded the building.

Q61: Our new sentence contains 5 words.

Q62: Betty's husband claimed a woman her age didn't need a racing car.

Q63: Since fifty-seven counts as 1 word, our sentence deleted 8 words.

Q64: Many ways to rewrite the sentence. Our version: Standing in his motel doorway, he held an envelope a female messenger had delivered. He watched her walk away.

Q65: She smiles at me.

Q66: I went back into the hotel. This sentences means the same thing and saves 3 words. Doesn't matter that he had to swing around to do this.

Q67: Joe reached toward me. This sentence means the same thing and saves 5 words. Doesn't matter what he had to do with his hands during the act of reaching.

Q68: Anna decided to leave. This sentence saves 13 words. Telling us she glared at Bob and then at the top of her father's head, is superfluous and has no value to the plot. It would have been vital if, say, her father suddenly grew three new sets of ears.

Q69: She walked to the window. This sentence saves 5 words. If she walked to the window, we don't have to be told she stood to do this. You can't walk unless you are standing. Also, what she did with her back is insignificant.

Q70: Nora peeked to see if Sam was coming. This sentence saves 5 words. Doesn't matter what Nora had to do with her head so she could peek outside. In fact, using the word twisted creates an odd visual.

Q71: He saw the boat sail by. Doesn't matter what part of his eye was used to do this.

Q72: A dainty woman approached me.

Q73: Joe was hallucinating.

Q74: Helen went to the park.

Q75: A number of ways to do this. Our version: When the sun rose, Nora crawled out of her boulder-protected cave.

Q76: The crowd laughed at the clown.

Q77: Frank ordered a drink.

Q78: Sam thought he'd throw up.

Q79: She got an idea.

Q80: Fred saw hatred in his eyes.

Q81: The car rolled toward them slowly.

Q82: She blushed.

Q83: Denny looked where she pointed and found a boy.

Q84: Harold didn't listen to Nancy's protest.

Q85: She was short.

Q86: He talked to himself because he was lonely.

Q87: As I walk, I smell something peculiar.

Q88: A number of ways to do this. Our version: He looked again at the main entrance.

Q89: A number of ways to do this. Our version: When Mary was fifteen, she made a secret pact with a rock star. He'd sent her an autographed picture she'd requested in a fan letter.

Q90: Citizens felt smothered by August's high humidity.

Q91: Trivial details are: *extremely, little thing with long brown tresses that dripped water on her cotton summer sundress.*

Q92: An SUV crushed my husband to death on Flag Day. This saves 27 words.

Q93: America is the greatest country in the world. This saves 10 words.

Q94: He sat on jungle foliage that covered an alley. This saves 27 words.

Q95: He heard a single aircraft.

Q96: She stopped at the bedroom door.

Q97: Flashbacks move the story backward. FF is supposed to move forward at all times, as quickly as possible.

Q98: She carved a pumpkin.

Q99: A number of ways to do this. Our version: Hank opened the envelope and saw a lawyer's signature on the letter inside.

Q100: A number of ways to do this. Our version: He went back to his room, put on a sweater, and went to the dark kitchen.

Q101: Sally removed a journal from her backpack.

Q102: Several ways to do this. Our version: He discarded the empty hypodermic needle cartridge in a trashcan.

Q103: He started the car and drove into the street.

Q104: Several ways to do this. Our version: Jean went to the open door and looked outside.

Q105: Several ways to do this. Our version. Leaving his car, Frank unlocked the bar's door, and went inside.

Q106: Several ways to do this. Our version: I went to Mary's table.

Q107: Harry left the jewelry store.

Q108: Lester didn't appreciate Bill's sarcasm.

Q109: Freddie was at the kitchen table, taking a quiz in her magazine.

ANSWERS FOR

WORD REDUCTION EXERCISES

Q01: He kept old tools in his workshop. Doesn't matter where the workshop is located.

Q02: He smiled. Saves 3 words.

Q03: He couldn't understand what his clients wanted. Saves 7 words.

Q04: He whimpered.

Q05: The woman looked startled.

Q06: I dropped the ice bucket and ran to my room.

Q07: I followed Bobby to his mansion.

Q08: Howling with pain, he collapsed on the pavement.

Q09: I opened my mouth but didn't speak.

Q10: The baker cowered.

Q11: I heard police sirens as they pulled into the hotel parking lot.

Q12: His rotting flesh smelled terrible.

Q13: Nothing was there.

Q14: When he left his car, I shot him in the head. No need to mention leaving him in a pool of blood, because that happens to everybody who dies this way.

Q15: The sword decapitated the vampire.

Q16: The clock said 2:33.

Q17: Rain pelted the house.

Q18: He decided to confront them.

Q19: He walked toward the door, but Ellie stopped him.

Q20: She fixed the problem.

Q21: Then he found a rotting lantern made from Landon's head.

Q22: Erika's face was long.

Q23: I arrived and put his body into the incinerator. Doesn't matter where the incinerator was located.

Q24: Raymond saw people laughing.

Q25: The pedestrians stopped walking.

Q26: The audience applauded louder.

Q27: Jack nodded.

Q28: She looked sick and exhausted.

Q29: She didn't answer, but pushed harder into the pulpy floor.

Q30: He let go and looked into his wife's eyes.

Q31: The audience stood and applauded the winner. If they're applauding, they are honoring.

Q32: Phil liked sweets and was cruel.

Q33: I thought I'd feel bad murdering somebody, but I was calm.

Q34: She fell asleep.

Q35: I took off my engagement ring and handed it to Johnny.

Q36: After drying her shoes, she put them on, and looked into the bathroom mirror. Doesn't matter exactly where the bathroom mirror was located.

Q37: He didn't mention his wife, but spoke of his daughters.

Q38: The old man on the sidewalk sputtered and waved. Doesn't matter what the distance was between them.

Q39: She was eccentric. Saves 5 words.

Q40: After vomiting, he stood.

Q41: No longer shocked, he felt disgusted.

Q42: I heard her cursing under her breath.

Q43: After screaming, he drove off.

Q44: Charlie consulted his science book.

Q45: A young attorney suddenly scurried out the door, looking terrorized.

Q46: Suddenly, she felt tired.

Q47: He kept licking his cracked bloody lips, not sure what was happening.

Q48: Rosie would hoot and laugh out loud. Dropped start to. If you start to do something, you're doing it.

Q49: She rarely smiled.

Q50: George was sitting quietly. Since this is in 1st person, it's assumed the protagonist sees everything that's going on. No need to remind readers what the protagonist sees with his eyes.

Made in the USA
Lexington, KY
09 June 2014